DID YOUR SON MARRY A PRINCESS?

By
Natalie B. Sedgewick

Dedication

I am so blessed to have met amazing women believers who have shared their struggles and hurtful situations.

I am so thankful for the women in my Bible Study in the Philippines who supported each other with our difficult situations.

For the women who have been in my Bible Studies over the years and in Life Groups who love the Lord and want to pray for each other.

I want to thank you for inspiring me and supporting me as I have put down on pages what we have faced that are not of our choosing.

I'm so thankful for my friends whom I've met in all my travels and moves, and became close friends and confidants who will always be in my heart forever.

Thank you, Laura, for proofreading, helping with suggestions, and being a loving Christian sister of faith.

But, most of all, I want to thank my daughter, who has encouraged me over the years to finally finish writing this book.

I love you and appreciate you for the beautiful woman you are in Christ.

Acknowledgment

To the families who have walked similar paths, your stories, prayers and quiet perseverance inspired me more than you will know. Many families face challenges like mine, where relationships grow complicated, and it is my hope that these reflections offer understanding, compassion and encouragement. To every reader who picks up this book—thank you for being willing to read a story of faith, family, and the lessons we learn along the way. My prayer is that these pages bring comfort, insight, and *hope.*

Foreword

Isaiah 43 is special. The Lord God of Israel was telling the Israelites, and it applies to us today, that He will get us through the difficulties of life. How powerful it is that God has shown Himself time and time again in my life, and that He alone can help me through tough times. He is my strength and my go-to when life is difficult and when it is hard to understand circumstances that feel impossible to cope with. I want to share with you how God has provided for and taken care of my family through the years. The events in our lives are what make us stronger and help us grow in our Lord. There have been times when I thought it could not get worse, but I have gone to His Word and found peace, comfort, and strength to carry on. He will provide for us and lead us through those difficult times that seem almost impossible. I have "hope" in Him, and I have taken that as my "buzz" word for my future. I have been encouraged to share some of my interesting life experiences with you.

I wrote a children's book at the time I started this one. However, I kept putting this one off. In the past few years, I have heard more and more stories about sons marrying difficult girls who become daughters-in-law and how these women, whom I call "Princesses," have torn families apart. These ongoing situations continue to hurt our hearts as parents and grandparents. My desire in writing this book was to share how God has helped me and others through these difficult times and the hurts that life throws at us. I also want to encourage others by showing how God can be our strength and healer when our hearts are broken. I am writing to share what it has been like to have a "Princess" for a daughter-in-law and how God can help us navigate these relationships through prayer, the Bible, and the support of friends.

Table of Contents

Introduction

I grew up in the 50s, the time of Walt Disney and his beloved films about princesses finding their true loves. Awwwww! The princesses were kind to everyone and everything, including those cute animated animals. These princesses had sweet dispositions, an aura of perfection, and, of course, were beautiful to the eye. All my little friends were going to the movie theater, and we only had one in town, to see these films, but sadly for me, I was not permitted to go. I grew up in a very strict, legalistic Christian home where movies were considered "sinful." I was not allowed to dance, which included the gym classes where everyone was taught square dancing. However, I sat on the side watching and feeling embarrassed because my mom wrote a note to the teacher saying it was against my religion to dance. Decks of cards were also considered a sin because the Joker was thought to be Satanic. Looking back at my childhood, I have wondered why my parents thought even going to a Disney movie could be considered bad. How could animated, colorful films be so terrible? Did not good overcome evil in all these movies? I do not think it was really the movies themselves, especially films like the Disney productions. Instead, the theater itself was considered "worldly," and it was believed that things happened in the back seats with guys and girls that should not be done in public. So, being the respectful child I was brought up to be, I did not question my parents. As an adult, I can look back and see that it was the time and the culture, and that my parents did the best they could with the tools they had during my upbringing. However, I felt heartbroken when my neighbor's playmate's mom asked me to go to the movies with them to see "Cinderella." Wow! I could not believe they had invited me to go, especially when it was not even discussed in my home. I ran into the house as fast as I could in anticipation of a positive answer, but instead, my mom simply said, "No," and explained that we did not believe in going to movies. Talk about disappointment! I was really bummed. As a child, it hurt deeply, and I was so disappointed that I could not see this colorful, beautifully illustrated movie about a girl who became a real princess. In my dreams, I thought that would be the most wonderful thing to happen to me or to any girl. As a young girl, I was able to read some of the stories from those Golden Books that everyone read in the 50s. They are actually still around, and I have read many of them to my preschool students.

I really enjoyed reading and had a great imagination for placing myself in these stories and pretending I was that poor girl who could become a beautiful princess. I imagined being transformed into beautiful gowns and wearing glass slippers. Maybe that was when I discovered that I loved shoes. Before I got married, when I was single and working, I had 50 pairs of shoes in my closet. I had a pair for every outfit and loved being different, so I had a variety of colors and styles. My poor aging feet regret some of those choices now, and my podiatrist reminds me each time I visit that I made some bad choices. When you have a "thing" for shoes when you are younger, you do not think about the condition of your feet in the future.

Going back to princesses, when I was growing up, a princess was something extremely "special." Every little girl wanted to marry her "Prince Charming" and live happily ever after. We all wanted to be real princesses who had beautiful, flowing gowns and glass slippers, lived in a huge, beautiful castle with everything imaginable, including people to wait on them. It seemed about as perfect as one could get to living a magical life. It was like a utopia where everything was perfect, and everyone was kind and loving. Do you remember dressing up in your mom's high heel shoes that were much too big? You would clomp around pretending they were glass slippers. Did you also put on your mom's dress so it could become a gown because it was so long on you? I remember having so much fun with my neighbor as we played "dress up."

Unfortunately, life is not like the "Disney movies" or the "Hallmark movies" or our childhood games of dress up. We rarely see someone marry a real prince, but I always loved the idea of a princess. Unfortunately, I have lost that ideal fantasy. With many families hurting today, I am part of the reality of the "new princesses" who are hurting families and breaking them apart. I want to share with you what has become the reality for families whose sons have married "princesses." I am hoping that those of you who read this book and can relate (I understand there are many now) will want to see what God says about our situation and how we can help and support each other. Eventually, I hope we can all come to have healthy relationships with our sons and their wives. "Hope" is our special word.

Hebrews 11:1 *"Now faith is confidence in what we hope for and assurance about what we do not see."*

Chapter 1
Princesses

There seems to be a growing number of young married women who come across as "princesses." They talk and act as if they are very "royal," as though everyone is beneath them because of their attitudes. The reality is that they can be cruel, unkind, selfish, and disrespectful. In the Bible, it specifically says to love, honor, and respect your parents. So how did our sons change their attitudes and behaviors toward us?

Colossians 3:20 *"Children, obey your parents in everything, for this pleases God."* It does not say only until you are married. I do not believe God intended that once you said, "I do," you were suddenly not to have a relationship with your parents, or that you should become extremely critical of everything your parents say or do. Well, it seems the change occurred after they were married to the Princesses.

We live in an imperfect world, and as such, we are not perfect people because of sin. However, there are young women in this world today who have married our sons and live in this fantasy world, believing and acting as though they are better than us. In the Bible, it states that we are all born in sin, and when we become believers, we are supposed to leave worldly ways behind. Worldly ways are anything that is contrary to the Bible, God's Holy Word, which we are supposed to try, at least as believers, to follow. We all make mistakes, and I know I can confess my sins and try to make better choices, as my Savior says I should do. I should consciously try to make those right choices. I have messed up many times, but I have a conscience that makes me try to do better as a believer in Christ. I do not understand why an effort to be honest, loving, and caring can be taken so negatively. I am totally alarmed, and I do not understand these women who profess to be true believers, who are actively involved in their churches, and who were raised in Christian homes with parents, siblings, and family around them, who profess to be truly women with values and leaders in their churches.

However, they continue to do the opposite in their relationships with their in-laws. They are wonderful actors and make people believe they are truly as wonderful as they think they are. They can stand up in front of a group of women in a church and profess to love God, know the Bible thoroughly, and advise their followers on how to be great women and mothers of faith. However, unlike my fairy tale princesses, these women can be harsh and unkind, even to the point of meanness, and especially selfish and controlling. I believe they imagine themselves to be so wonderful, so thoughtful, so loving, and very respectful that most people do not see through their veneer. Even if the husbands do see these two sides, they are often either unaware of the behavior, as the old saying goes, "love is blind," or they choose to ignore it because they are married to these women. They have to live with these girls 24/7, so it is natural to understand that the wives will be first and foremost in their lives. However, I am of the opinion that these girls believe in their own minds that they are so "perfect" that no one, heaven forbid, should ever say anything negative about anything that concerns their little world. In fact, you should not dare to say anything that could even be interpreted as negative because of the reaction you may receive or the actions that can be taken against you, such as claiming you are not trusted to be with the grandchildren and therefore have no rights to them. We know of a couple who took their daughter-in-law to court to secure their rights as grandparents and won. The women I have spoken to about this have all agreed that grandparents do have rights to see their grandchildren, and in some states, as I mentioned about this couple, you can actually go to court. These princesses believe that they should have everything their way, and their wishes are that they deserve to have their heart's desires regardless of hurting others. They are very skilled at deceiving people with their winning smiles and the appearance of a generous and loving façade. They make YouTube videos, write books, and claim to be devoted Christians who are knowledgeable about the Bible, yet they appear to ignore its teachings, which not only hurts others but also harms themselves in the end.

There are also some daughters-in-law who are not Christians and have never had a relationship with God, and they too can be just as hurtful and have the attitude that our generation is ignorant and does not understand the new way of relationships with in-laws.

In doing some research, I found a definition called "the daughter-in-law syndrome." The Mother-in-Law Daughter-in-Law Syndrome emerges when the two female members of the household fail to establish rapport, resulting in tension that detrimentally impacts the overall home atmosphere. While these issues have historically existed, they have become more and more conspicuous in today's evolving times. This is a quote from the Mumsnet chat.

I recently watched a YouTube video that was spot on about daughters-in-law and mothers-in-law. Basically, the mother-in-law is sitting across from the daughter-in-law, and they are having a conversation about the grandchild. The daughter-in-law is accusing the mother-in-law of not following their rules, and she pulls out a book that is six inches thick. The mother-in-law defends herself by saying that the role of a grandparent is to spoil the child, to love them, and to make them feel special. The son comes into the room and is supposed to defend his wife when the mom says that she baked chocolate chip cookies that are on the kitchen counter. He dashes off without helping the situation. Finally, the daughter-in-law criticizes the poor woman for every little thing she does and sits there totally angry at the poor woman, who only wants to love her grandchild. However, because she is not following the Book of Rules, she is not allowed to have a relationship with the grandchild. Does any of this sound familiar?

I know there are some really sweet ladies who are married to our sons who are so sweet, thoughtful, and would not intentionally hurt their husbands' families. I have friends my son's age who are wonderful girls who would never hurt and tear apart families by their attitudes and behavior. However, there is a growing number of girls who are intentionally hurtful and are ending relationships with their husbands' families for whatever reason. So, for any of you who are reading this and know you are making the right choices, I can honestly commend you for it and hope that you will not take offense. I am not grouping everyone together.

I am just responding to the many who have shared their stories with me and want help in dealing with their daughters-in-law. I have spoken to counselors who deal with the increasing number of sessions about this topic.

Maybe your son has married a princess. You may very well relate to this subject matter that I am about to share, because it seems to be becoming more and more the norm with families. A friend's son had just moved to a new community with a new job and decided to attend a local church. The son had a career change and was getting older, and he thought he was ready to find a partner in life, a nice Christian girl who fulfilled his ideas. Apparently, "The Princess" saw him first and decided at that moment that she was going to marry him, even though they had not even been introduced. Is that how it happens in the Disney fairy tales? I think that kind of goes along with her actions. Needless to say, she definitely used her "princess charms," and within six months, she had a ring on her finger. Within a few months, there was to be her "perfect" wedding. Years later, the friend and her husband were informed that they ruined her wedding because of some ridiculous notions that left them dumbfounded.

They were never aware of this due to a lack of communication on the part of the princess, and she was still holding a grudge against them for something they were never even aware of at the time. To be honest, the issues were insignificant in the big scheme of things in life. We have all heard that "communication" is the most significant thing in any relationship, or even when planning events such as a wedding. If there is little communication, then what is going to happen? You are probably blamed for ruining the whole wedding from start to finish. It is the littlest things that can send the princess into a tizzy. Have you ever thought you were doing the right things, only to be told later that you were never doing the right things according to the princess?

Abigail had a son who brought the Princess to their home for the first time before he asked her to marry him. They arrived at the airport, where Abigail and her husband picked them up. As you can imagine, there were many questions in the back of her mind. What kind of girl was he bringing to their home? Was she going to be as nice as the previous girls he had dated? Would she be the kind of girl who would want to be a part of their family as much as her own?

Would she be willing to follow the son wherever God led, and would she always be supportive of him in every aspect of his life, including accepting his family?

Maybe you experienced these same thoughts when you were introduced to your son's possible partner in life. I think my friend and I thought it was normal to think these things since he had not really talked about her much, and they believed they were simply meeting a friend.

Have you ever had a time when your son was dating someone you thought would be absolutely perfect for him? As parents, we all want the best possible partner for our sons' lives. We absolutely loved the girl we thought our son was going to marry. They had met in college and were dating steadily. Over the course of time, I think he was struggling with many things in his life, including the stress of college life. Sadly, the day came when he called us to say they had broken up. I knew he was very serious about this girl, and we adored her. She went with us to meet our son in L.A. when he was working on an internship one summer during college. We spent just a couple of days with them, but she was so down-to-earth, completely sweet, and connected with us. We enjoyed going around the city seeing different sights, and we truly enjoyed her company. She accepted us as we accepted her, and we had high hopes that they would marry. He later told us that he actually had money saved for an engagement ring, but when they broke up, he went out and spent the money on some crazy item. So, we knew he had spent the money he had saved for the engagement ring. I think he was quite torn up about the breakup for a long time, and we were just as sad because we could have seen her as a wonderful daughter-in-law. We knew just by being around her that she was a genuine person and would have loved us as her in-laws unconditionally. However, what we think and want and what God has planned are often quite different, and it became obvious that God had a plan that was to include the Princess in our future. Our daughter-in-law lives in a bubble. She grew up in the same place, attended the same church, had the same family members around her, and went to the same private Christian school throughout all her school years, so she was always surrounded by the same friends. She never had an eye for seeing the bigger picture of the world around her, and because of that, she was raised very differently from our son. So, as you read, you may see why these differences had an effect on the relationship with the in-laws.

God sometimes pulls what I call "funnies," and we are not quite sure what, why, or with whom, but He has something in it for us that we may not understand at the time. However, it is always for our good. We may not always understand at the time, but eventually we see the "why."

I find myself wondering why things happened that caused the breakup with a girl we knew would make our lives richer and would not do hurtful things like keeping our grandchildren away from us or being spiteful and hurtful like the one he married. I am sure my parents and every set of parents often go through this. They think they know what is best and whom their sons should marry. I am certain my parents felt that way when I told them I was engaged to my husband. Maybe they did not think he was the right choice for me. I do know that my parents were prayer warriors, and I am sure they were praying for the best for me as their daughter. I appreciate my parents who loved me unconditionally and tried to do their best as parents. I know that though they are no longer with me, they are looking down and saying that God had a good plan for me. I am grateful that my husband would make them proud for the ways he has been such a good father to our children and supportive of his family. It is not "my ways" but God's ways, and whatever happened, God was in control of my son's life. I have to accept that there are things I cannot control, but God says to keep my focus on Him and not on the situation we are in. Believing that God chose a girl for my son and that she makes him totally happy and loves him unconditionally, then I am glad for him. Unfortunately, whenever we have had the limited times to be around my son since he married her, all I see is my son exhausted from taking care of the house and children while also working a high-pressure job to provide for his family, with many signs that all is not always wonderful living with the Princess.

Going back to Abigail, who was waiting to meet her son and the Princess in the luggage area, there he was walking with a very tall, slender, attractive blonde. She carried herself well and dressed very fashionably. Abigail thought to herself that they made a good-looking pair. They are both so tall and slender. Many people have said that her son is very handsome and could easily have posed for magazines or shopping catalogs. As she watched them walking toward them, she could only think of both of them posing on the cover of some fashion magazine. I thought it was okay for Abigail to voice her opinion about her "handsome" son. So, they drove home and enjoyed a home-cooked meal, and all seemed to be going quite well. She was just so happy to have some time with her son. The Princess was willing to be helpful and interact with them in conversation.

The Princess seemed comfortable and at ease, considering they were strangers who had just met. She was friendly and seemed so sweet and loving toward their son. She was excited that they attended a church led by one of her favorite pastors and could not wait to attend church that weekend with them. Abigail thought she must have been brought up in a good, faith-based home. In sharing her background, they discovered she was brought up in a Christian home and attended a Christian church school throughout her school years. She went to a local college, graduated, and had a job in a local business. She was also established in her career, and Abigail got the feeling she was seeking to get married. She was at an age when most of her friends were probably married, so maybe her eyes were set on their son. Abigail was alone in her kitchen when her son came out to join her. He asked her what she thought of his "friend." She honestly had only been around her for a few hours, not even a full day, but she said she seemed really nice. But in her gut, my friend was concerned. After all, he had not brought home a girl since he moved away. So, she had a feeling something big was about to be said. He put on a huge grin and said, "I'm going to ask her to marry me." He went on to explain that this girl had so much in common with her. He said she was like her in that she loved cooking, baking, crafts, and had other similar interests. She was a girl of faith, and he was going to ask her to marry him. Abigail appreciated that he thought enough of her at that time to say the girl was like her. It was very flattering, do you not think? She said, "I hope that you will be very happy." Well, she kind of wished she had been more like her, at least around them, because my friend said she would never have treated people, especially her husband's parents, the way she has treated them since the wedding day. At that very moment, Abigail knew things would never be the same again. Her sweet baby boy, her precious son, was a man, and he was going to leave his parents and become a spouse and the head of his own household. She understood it. We all understand it. He was ready for a commitment; he had found the one he wanted to spend his life with, and they understood. My friend and her husband were open and willing to accept her into their family. What bothered them was how fast things moved from that day, and they wondered if he had taken the time to really get to know her and discover the real person she was inside before making a permanent commitment.

Genesis 2:24 *"That is why a man leaves his father and mother and is united to his wife, and they become one flesh."*

When we get married to our husbands, we know that we are starting a new life as the two God planned, but it was not perceived that way by Abigail's son's "Princess." Later in the relationship, she actually accused her husband and Abigail of not understanding the concept of a husband leaving his parents to cleave to his wife. Yes, according to her, they did not understand that the two of them were one and that anything said was said to both of them. After that, Abigail was not allowed to talk to her son without the Princess around or have conversations without the Princess listening. I do know that after they were married, she was positive the Princess read his emails and all his texts on his phone. In fact, to this day, they are sure she listens to conversations he has and checks his emails and text messages, especially those from them, because of his inability to have communication with them. But I am absolutely sure, as a woman myself, that Abigail's son's princess has had many conversations with her mom and sisters without their son's presence or knowledge. It is just in our nature as females to talk to other girls or our moms, whereas guys tend to keep things to themselves. They tend to stay in their little "boxes." Yes, of course, it is in the Bible as God's plan for a husband and wife and how it is supposed to work. However, her perception was definitely different as it relates to relationships.

So, before I proceed into the relationships of daughters-in-law, I want to share that the women who have spoken with me are really nice people. Do you believe that you are considered someone who is very well-liked? Have you gotten along with everyone you have ever worked with, and from people's comments, can you say that you are "likeable"? Are you considered loyal, honest, and trustworthy, and not one to gossip? I am someone who does not like to ruffle feathers and usually keeps my comments to myself. In fact, I do not like conflict and avoid it at all costs. Confrontation sends me into a shell where I want to hide from the world. I will go out of my way to try to make things as positive as possible, even if I get hurt in the end. Yes, it can be detrimental, and I finally learned many years ago, after someone took advantage of me, that I do have to speak up for myself. I say all of this just to explain that these Princesses assume the worst about you. In their minds, you are not likeable or nice.

So, in my situation with my daughter-in-law, I finally spoke up under the supervision of a Christian counselor. The four of us decided to meet with someone who was an impartial party. We sat there in her office being attacked, and I think I finally snapped. The Princess decided that even though she had been hurtful since day one of their marriage, she was in the right and chose to blame us for everything. She then withdrew herself, the children, and our son after the meeting. The fact is that the truth hurts, and I finally said how her actions did not reflect what she professed. Looking back, I am sure I said things that I later regretted, but then I think it would not have mattered. As you know, when you say something that stings, you regret it and think, "Where did that come from?" or "That is not me at all." But after I kept hearing all these allegations from someone who had hardly spent any time with me and had already made up her mind before their marriage that she did not like me or his family, in that moment, she had pushed the buttons to the point that nothing was going to make things better. The daughter-in-law finally had the upper hand in controlling the relationship as she withdrew all contact with us. I wonder if there are other women out there who have had a similar experience where the daughter-in-law decides the fate of your relationship with your son and grandchildren. I did some research on the internet, which has a vast amount of information regarding this subject of daughters-in-law. One person said, and I quote, "I have always been nice to my daughter-in-law and never interfered, but she has always disliked me and now prefers my grandson to spend more time with her family than ours." Yes, our "princess" has always done this with our grandchildren since they were born. I assure you, there are many of you who can relate.

Another sweet lady, Tara, whom I have known for a long time, had this to share with me about her daughter-in-law.

Her son married a girl whose parents were hippies from the 60s. The daughter-in-law was the oldest child and had always been bitter that she had to practically raise the younger siblings. So, when her son and wife had their first child, she had Down syndrome. The wife became bitter about it and even said that it was everyone's responsibility to take care of a special child. In fact, when she was born, Tara went for a visit and was asked to leave for a day.

The daughter-in-law has had several falling outs with close friends, ending relationships, and is generally a very negative person. So, when Tara and her husband went to visit, things did not go well. Once, while my friend was playing with her granddaughter, the daughter-in-law simply took the child from her for no reason. On another visit, they had her stay at a friend's house instead of their own. The daughter-in-law did not want her at their house all the time.

During the first years of their marriage, they went to visit their son. It was the daughter's first day of kindergarten. The daughter-in-law instead went camping for the week. She totally missed her own daughter's first day of school.

Tara's son had been married for a while, and they had some problems, actually to the point that he left her. However, the daughter-in-law said that she would change. During a conversation, Tara even told the Princess that she loved her because her son loved her. The Princess was "insulted" because in her mind, she was not loved for herself. Tara had not even been given time to actually know her, but she was trying hard to have a relationship. Unfortunately, the Princess is very edgy all the time and defensive toward my friend and her husband. If they say or do anything positive, it is taken negatively. It is hard to understand why this daughter-in-law is so disrespectful and unkind to my friend and her husband.

Shortly after my son was married, they came for a short visit. Truly, I can count on one hand how many times they actually came to visit us together. Twice with her, and once he came alone because she did not want to come. It was interesting because we wondered what had happened to that sweet girl he had brought home for us to meet. Oh yes, she was just trying to impress us that first time, obviously. The real Princess finally showed her true colors when she did visit. She was aloof, hardly spoke, claimed a headache most of the time, and stayed in the bedroom talking to her mom or siblings on her cellphone. When we took them to the airport to leave, I gave my son a huge hug and tried to hold back the tears as he was leaving, as I did not know when I would see him again. Would you not be teary-eyed if you had not seen your son for months, and he was leaving, and you did not know when you would see him again? I believe that is called "normal."

Later, my son told me that she said I was "too emotional." Wow, this is the girl who had my grandchildren, and as a mom, she shows no emotion? Oh, and this was only the beginning of the constant negative comments about myself and my husband. For years, we have only been told the absolute hateful things we have done wrong, and we were "so demanding." We have never demanded anything, but obviously, they think so. These are excuses when they do not want you around.

Romans 8:1 *"Therefore, there is now no condemnation for those who are in Christ."* Unfortunately, we have only heard condemnation since the day they got engaged.

My son is creative, very talented, smart, and really wanted to make his engagement special. So, he made this amazing plan for how he was going to present her with the ring. Because he was always close to us at that time, he asked us if we would please come out and be a part of the engagement he had so meticulously planned. How do you say no to your son when he wants you, his parents, to be included? Of course, we would love to be a part of this special event. Oh my. To this day, I believe this was probably the biggest mistake we made because I truly believe she resented us being present when the Princess received her engagement ring. It was probably the start of the resentment, the hostility, and the hatefulness aimed toward his parents, although it was later carried over to his only sister as well.

Having sons, you have probably realized that they just do not "get it" sometimes. I attribute this situation to the fact that it was an entirely new situation for him. He had never asked a girl to marry him before the Princess. In actuality, he thought it was a perfectly wonderful idea for us to be a part of the engagement, and we thought so too. Probably other girls would have had no problem with his parents being there, or even her parents, but then again, maybe it was our big mistake in going. I guess it was tragically a mistake we cannot do over. My husband and I took pictures of it happening, something they would not have had otherwise, and they were both so giddy and so much in love that it appeared to us that it did not matter that we were there except to observe the happy occasion. She was showing everyone her ring and telling people that they had just gotten engaged.

Sometime later, he did mention to us that he had invited her parents, but they declined because it was "her" special time. Yes, a big guilt trip was laid on us. I guess we made a huge mistake in her eyes, even though everyone we knew thought it was wonderful and so thoughtful of our son to want us to be a part of this event in his life. Which leads me to a question that bothers me. If she truly loves my son, why would it really matter that we were there, and why hurt our son by being so hateful to his parents? Do his feelings even matter to her? Sorry, that was two questions!

I was given this situation for you to relate to. Have you ever thought about times when you hope God is working good things out, and then you become disappointed and do not understand why? It is hard to explain the feelings that went through Michelle's mind when she and her family met the family of the Princess. There had been great hopes that they would be friendly and make everyone feel welcome. This was especially a time when things were not the best financially for them, and it meant spending money on flights to go back and forth for the upcoming wedding. As you know, we all have ups and downs in our life's financial journey, and sometimes the funds are just not what you would like them to be, especially when events like this happen. But we all do what we need to do to make it work. Michelle knew they needed to do this for their son, so they made the arrangements for a hotel, flights, a rental car, and, of course, meals during the time they were there for this meeting and eventually the wedding. I am sure this never even crossed their son's mind, but they knew that no matter what the circumstance, this was their only son and he was getting married. He probably did not understand, though, why his mom did not fly out to attend the wedding shower, although a gift was sent. Actually, no written shower invitation was received, only a verbal invitation through the son. But honestly, even if it had not been the cost involved, it was the fact that they did not feel at all comfortable around her or her family.

Michelle's family flew out and were told that they were meeting the soon-to-be daughter-in-law's parents and some siblings at a restaurant. It turned out to be a country club restaurant, and there was a long table with her parents and siblings on one side, and the son's family was seated on the other side.

They were asked to sit down on the other side of this long table facing them.

Did I mention it was a long table? I do not know how you would feel in this situation, but Michelle told me they all felt like it was a court trial, and the daughter-in-law's family were the jury while they were on the defense. Yes, that is pretty much her interpretation of the event. Her parents may not have even thought of it that way, and she would give them the benefit of the doubt that they were trying to be kind, but that was the perception of the event. No one else was around except the wait staff. There were long gaps of silence as they struggled to find something in common to discuss. Awkward. It was an uncomfortable situation. Then Michelle said her mind started wandering, and she began to feel anxious. Have you ever felt that way in a situation? Our crazy brains are trying to figure everything out. Maybe they were not good enough. Did they already not like them? What is wrong with us, she asked herself. Do they not like the way we talk or dress? Michelle told me that she had never felt so uncomfortable in her life as she sat there wondering if they thought their son was good enough for their daughter. Bear in mind, the Princess was the eldest of the siblings, but they were all grown and in high school or college, so it was not like they were young parents with small children. However, the Princess was the first to get married. They suffered through this long and painful lunch with people they had never met, who made them feel like they were foreigners from another country. Michelle shared that she honestly feels her family has always been made to feel like they were not up to their standards. Of course, they may have had similar thoughts about them, but she knows she is pretty good at reading people through their words and actions, and they all felt that they did not really care for them. Was it because they were not residents of the state where they had always lived? Was it because they were not of the same church affiliation? But wait a minute, are we not all supposed to be part of the "family of Christ" no matter what church we attend? You could reason it out for decades and still not have the answers. They made it through the ordeal and returned home to wait for information about what was expected for the upcoming wedding that would take place in the summer, just a few months away.

Now the trouble really started with "The Princess." Wedding plans.

Chapter 2
Time Warp

At this point, I'm going to go back in time and give you some background about my son and how he grew up. I'd like to share with you that his "Princess" grew up very differently. As I mentioned before, she was raised in the same city all her life. She has always been around her extended family with aunts, uncles, grandparents, and cousins. She also attended the same church where not only her parents, but generations of the family were raised. She has had the same friends since childhood.

I love Star Trek and all those sci-fi programs that could send a person back in time in a single "zap" as you are transported to a different time or place. Since I do like that idea, I decided that I'd like to share with you the background of where my son came from and how his upbringing was much different than his Princess's. Also, I feel maybe sharing some of our life experiences may help in understanding how my son was raised, and I want to share how God, time and time again, has gotten us through some pretty stressful events. Maybe going into the background of my life experiences may also help you understand why I'm writing this book. Over the years, people have asked about our lives, the travel, living in a foreign country, and living in so many places and cultures. My hope is that by sharing my personal life experiences, you might see that you are definitely not alone, as we all face difficult times in this journey. I have always tried to put my relationship with Jesus as the first and most important in my life. I know as a mom I made mistakes and wish that I could erase some things I said or did that might not have honored God. But I also know I serve a God who forgives and that He has forgiven me. God put it on my heart to share because not only has my son married one of these women, but there are many of you going through this same situation of hurt and confusion as to why you are being treated so poorly. In fact, my siblings have sons who married "princesses" who have divided their families and caused undue heartbreak to their parents and siblings. I have been encouraged to write this by dear people in my life who matter because I know there are many hurting families, maybe like you, who have seen this behavior among these girls. When asked about my topic, it's interesting how it makes women open up to me about their similar situations.

In fact, today I was told about a similar situation of a Princess in the family, and she said that over and over they say and think, "don't lose sight of the big picture." These couples lose sight of what life is really all about, not selfishness and pride. Life is too short to be so disrespectful to families on both sides. We even had a discussion with a Christian counselor who told us that we are not alone in this situation, as there are countless families today who are being divided by these same kinds of women I call "princesses." On one of the chats, I read this: "My DIL is totally possessive with my son and doesn't like him to visit us." We can relate to this, as these "princesses" do seem to be very possessive. Anyways, let us continue and let me start from the beginning....

Chapter 3
Son's Roots

I believe God has a purpose for each one of our lives. We can look to Him for guidance and direction about everything that concerns our lives. I married young. My husband was only 19 and a local boy who came from a dysfunctional family. Thankfully, my close relationship with the Lord brought him to church with me, and he became a believer before we were engaged. I was very firm that I would only marry a Christian man. I think my parents had a mixture of emotions about our engagement. They knew his background and his family, so they never said anything to me directly, but I knew in the back of their minds they were worried about whether I was making the right choice. I didn't have a doubt that he was the one God had chosen for me, and even with all the ups and downs, we've been married many years, so I guess God had it right. Truly, it has taken faith, hope, forgiveness, and Christ as the center of our lives, being grounded in Him when we have been thrown into difficult circumstances. We planned to be married in May when he had graduated from junior college. I was working as a secretary (administrative assistant now) in the engineering department of a large company. I had wanted to marry in May because I love the beauty of spring in the Northeast, the colors, the emerging flowers, and the smell of clean, fresh air after a rainfall. Besides that, being in the North, the winters are usually snowy, slushy, muddy, salt, dirty, and overcast skies most of the time. (Maybe that's why we settled in the South!)

However, my mother-in-law, who was going through the process of divorcing his father (wasn't that fun trying to plan a wedding with that going on, not!), decided she was moving to California, and she wanted to see us married before she moved. So, instead of the wedding I thought I would have, we had to plan the wedding for January during his semester break from college and around her plans. I was raised to respect my elders, so I felt I should definitely comply with her wishes. (I wonder how my son's Princess would have reacted if I had been demanding with her?) His mother also insisted that I have her younger sister as one of my bridesmaids, as well as his younger brother. Again, it was really hard for me to comply, but I thought at the time I needed to because I was going to be a part of his family. (I will interject here that I don't see much respect anymore regarding older people or those in authority, so this would probably not happen today.) Besides, she was going to be my mother-in-law, and I wanted to make sure she liked me and had no doubt that I was going to make her son happy. In my mind, I was young and very naive, but I was hoping to have that fairy-tale life with a wonderful new family.

Well, out the door went the beauty of spring that I had hoped for on our wedding day! It turned out to be a major "nor'easter," as we say in the Northeast of the U.S., when major storms rush across the country and then turn up toward the northeastern part of the U.S. So, starting early that morning, the large, puffy white flakes just kept coming down fast and furious. Unfortunately, when it was time for the ceremony, there was nothing but a blanket of white everywhere. It was blowing and swirling around like crazy, and visibility was minimal for driving. If you have ever grown up in the North, where winters can be harsh, and driving can be almost impossible at times, then you will understand that many of the guests were not able to come because of those conditions. All the wedding party, local friends and family managed to get to the church. The flowers were delivered amazingly, and even our two ministers were there, and the ceremony went off as planned. During the ceremony, the roads were being cleared, but the snow was still falling. In the North, they know how to clear roads with plows and sand and salt the roads that are slick, which is not the case in most of the southern cities we have lived in.

Afterwards, the reception was held in the church hall, where our small-town church held all its activities. Some of the sweet ladies of the church had prepared and decorated the hall, and it turned out to be a very lovely little reception. However, during the reception, my now mother-in-law, who I can say in all honesty was very strong-minded, strong-willed, and difficult to deal with at times, but was loved through Christ, informed us that she had decided not to move to California and was staying in town. Ugh! Did she really feel it was a good time to inform us that she was living very close to us? This was supposed to be my special day, and then we received that news. To top it off, when we left the church to change, my beautiful wedding dress was stained with mud, and of course, my beautiful white satin shoes were goners, stained with salt and dirty slush, never to be worn again. Now you know why I liked the month of May!!

The day was coming to a close, and we went on to our honeymoon, which was supposed to be only about a four-hour drive. However, we were driving in the horrible snowstorm that had covered most of the state. We were driving in it for hours and hours in the dark, with low visibility from the falling snow, which was beginning to drift across the unfamiliar roads. During this travel, we didn't have a GPS, cellphones, or any other technology. We had what we called a "map," a large (not easy to manipulate in a very small space) piece of paper filled with numerous lines that represented roads. My new husband came to realize that I did not know how to read a map. So, around midnight, in the little red VW Beetle, we were basically the only ones on the road except for the snowplow that we followed. We saw many cars in ditches and were very thankful the little "Bug," with its rear-wheel drive, had kept us chugging along. I realized that we had missed the exit, and it took a lot longer to get to the resort, but we finally made it and thanked the Lord for His care! Thinking back, I really loved that little Super Beetle by VW. It was a cute, bright red with black stripes to make it look really cool. I know I didn't tell you that I have a passion for cars. As a young girl, I knew every make and model of vehicles on the road, and I could even change the oil by learning from watching my brother, as he always had a hobby for cars. Maybe that's why I drive a sporty car today!

Upon returning to our hometown, my new husband went back to school, and I went back to work. Unfortunately, we found ourselves with his mom wanting to run our lives. That was when I decided that when my children got married, I would absolutely not be an interfering mother-in-law. Although The Princess and my son are of the mindset that I am one, my husband and I have never interfered with our son's upbringing of his children, or asked about finances, or done anything that would cause us to be labeled as such. In fact, due to my own mother-in-law, I have always been extremely cautious about what I even say to my son or his wife about any topic. I may have a bloody tongue from biting it so many times around The Princess, but I didn't speak my mind until the counseling session that went very badly. Mothers-in-law get so stereotyped, thanks to movies, books, etc., as always meddling and interfering with their children, so I have strived to never be that kind of in-law. But apparently, my daughter-in-law, The Princess, believes otherwise. Kudos to those of you who are not the interfering kind, because we apparently are "labeled" anyway.

We'd only been married three months when one day my husband came home from his classes and told me that he had decided to join the Army. What??????? I had always lived in this small town, grown up in my small church with all my friends, and all my siblings were there. My sister and older brother were married with their own children, and, of course, my parents were there. I didn't want to leave my comfort zone! I understood that he was trying to make a better life for us. At the time, the Army was offering incentives for paying college expenses. But the biggest reason was that he wanted us to move away from his mother's interference, the small-town life, and make a better future for us and our eventual children. I prayed about it, he prayed about it, and we felt like it was the right thing to do. Besides, I felt it was my purpose, according to the Bible, to follow my husband wherever he needed to go to provide for us. I thought of Ruth when she said to Naomi, *"Where you go, I will go, and where you stay, I will stay."* **Ruth 1:16**. (Let me interject that The Princess told our son before they got married that she was not willing to move even if his job took him to another place. However, she might consider the next state, but that was as far as she'd go. This was one of many warning signs he did not see.)

My husband finished school and got his AA degree, and then he enlisted in the Army that June. I continued to work while he went to basic training and advanced training, and finally, he got his orders to report to Fort Knox, KY, and become a soldier. He came back on leave for us to move at Christmas. So, I was able to find us an apartment near the base. We found out later that we were blessed, thank you Lord again, that this apartment complex was mostly officers, so it was truly a nice and safe place to live for us. At that time, we owned a very cute little two-seater sports car with a convertible top. Needless to say, that was not a practical vehicle for our move to another state, actually several states away from our home. We decided that our car was not suitable for travel, so we went shopping and got another sporty car, a Mustang Mach 1 fastback. Practical, not so much. When you're young, you don't always know how to make the best choices, right? But we managed to cram our basics into that car, and the rest of our few belongings were put on a commercial moving truck that was making several other small pickups like ours. Little did we realize, another thing you learn from experience, was that it was going to take a month before we ever saw our bed, couch, and other items we had in our apartment, as well as pots and pans, dishes, etc. We left on the day after Christmas and, with tears and apprehension, we traveled to his new assignment and began a new life together.

Chapter 4
First Move

What surprised me was that we had only been in the apartment a week when he was sent to "the field" for a week. Oh, and it was not just that week, but every other week for months and months. I didn't know anyone and had only said "hello" to some of the other tenants. I was alone, scared, and angry, a basketful of emotions because he had brought me away from the security of my home to live in a place where I knew no one and, worse, cockroaches. Big, black, ugly bugs that did not belong in my apartment, but they were there anyway. I had never seen such awful bugs before. Did you know they can jump? We slept on the floor for that month while we waited for our belongings to arrive. I still remember how hard it was to sleep for fear that one of those black, ugly bugs would crawl on me during the night. Yes, I was not a happy soldier's wife. I can still remember hearing the neighbors next door fighting, and sometimes I would get scared, wondering what was really going on.

I had never lived in an apartment before, so I was not used to hearing doors banging at all hours, people talking loudly in the breezeway, and hearing words I had really never heard before. Remember, I told you I was naïve. Small-town girl, small-town church, small-town thinking. We had a small TV sitting on a box, and for the first time, I started watching "soap operas." It became a place to lose myself and not think about how miserable and lonely I was at that time. Also, even though I had experience as a secretary, I was not able to find a job. Although I tried for months, I was told that because my husband was a soldier, the possibility of us moving caused employers to refrain from hiring anyone who was married to someone in the military. I truly felt that God was putting me through tests that I had never experienced before in my life.

The "field" became an every-other-week occurrence that I had to simply accept as part of military life. Finally, our bed and other belongings arrived, and I had at least a project for myself, putting our little home together and making it feel more comfortable. One evening, about two months after we had moved there, he was out in the field when we had tornado warnings across the area. I had never experienced a tornado before, and living in the north, you just don't usually deal with them. So, I sat in the upper-floor apartment with the terrible weather raging outside, scared to death for myself but also worried about my husband, who was out doing field exercises. Suddenly, I heard a knock on the door. I opened it as wind and rain pounded loudly outside, and it was the neighbor who lived below us. He kindly asked if I wanted to join them for dinner since I was alone. Thank you, Lord. It is amazing how God knows the right time and place to answer prayers. This couple later turned out to be good friends. Ed was a soldier at the base as well, and his wife was a sweet Midwest girl who loved to say "hells bells," a phrase I had never heard before. I hardly knew them except for passing by their lower apartment on our way up to ours, but they were warm and gracious and kindly asked me to stay until the storms blew over. They were from Indiana and were very used to tornado warnings. They decided we should play cards as we waited out the storms together. As we sat with candles lit because the power had gone out, we suddenly heard a strange sound. She told me to listen carefully as a noise like a train grew louder. She calmly said, "Oh, that's the tornado across the road from us following the river." Wow. Another first experience for this northerner. Thank goodness it was across the road and not directly on us. The next day, my husband returned home and shared stories about the damage caused by the terrible weather.

I had no idea that tornadoes could cause so much destruction. As a brave soldier, he first tried to make it sound like being out in the field when the tornado hit the area was not too bad, but then he admitted his fear and explained that it had truly been a frightening experience that night. We were both deeply grateful and thankful that God had kept us safe.

I became pregnant with my first child and was so happy and excited. Around my fourth month of pregnancy, I began having back problems and some bleeding. I was scheduled to fly home because my husband was going to be doing a military exercise in the state of Wisconsin, which was a long way away. I went to the OB/GYN clinic on base, where I had been receiving my prenatal care. I was planning to fly home that week to stay the summer with my parents while he was away. However, I still was not feeling well, so I made an appointment to see the Army doctor. He examined me and said it was fine for me to fly. My husband took me to the airport the next morning, as he was leaving the following day. We were both anxious about being apart for so long and concerned because I was not feeling well. On the other hand, I was going "home" to see my parents for the first time since we had moved away. The plane took off, and suddenly I felt a surge of pressure in my lower abdomen. This was the first time I had ever flown alone and only the second time I had ever been on a plane. To this day, I still have a deep fear of flying alone and avoid doing so whenever possible.

I remembered the bathroom was at the back of the plane, so as soon as the seatbelt sign turned off, I focused only on trying to get there. However, as I walked down the aisle, blood was running down my legs. I quickly got the attention of a flight attendant who took one look at my condition and hurried me to the back of the plane. Everything became a blur, but I remember she asked passengers to move from the seats in the last row, put the armrests up, and helped me lie down. I recall the pilot asking over the intercom if there was a doctor on the flight. Soon, a gentleman came to the back, looked at me lying there, and said, "I'm not an OB doctor, but I'm pretty sure she is miscarrying."

When we landed in the city where I was supposed to change planes and continue my trip, I was taken off the aircraft and transferred to an ambulance. I did not even realize there were special ways of exiting a plane like that, but they carefully removed me so the other passengers would not see me. I was taken to the nearest hospital, and after an examination, a female doctor explained that she would have to perform a D&C because I was miscarrying.

I was alone and frightened. However, I felt a deep peace that I am sure came from the Holy Spirit. After the procedure, the doctor gently explained that it was a blessing in disguise because the fetus had been severely deformed. Even so, I was devastated. I remember crying and feeling incredibly alone. A staff member took me to a shared hospital room where a kind woman was resting in the other bed. She showed genuine concern for me and treated me with great compassion. I appreciated that she did not ask many questions and simply offered quiet comfort. I was placed in an area designated for women undergoing gynecological procedures and not in the maternity ward, which I was thankful for.

I did not know where my husband was or whether he had even been informed. I had no idea what I was going to do next or whether I should continue on to my family. Then, around midnight, I saw him standing in the doorway. Somehow, the airline had contacted my husband's commander, who compassionately arranged for him to be located before his unit departed the base and sent him on a flight to Pittsburgh with emergency leave. In that moment, I felt overwhelming gratitude, knowing my Savior always understands my needs and cares for me in every situation.

We were able to fly home for a couple of days before returning to our house. What a comfort it was to be with my family again, especially after what had just happened. There is nothing better for comfort than your mom. Unfortunately, my son has lost sight of the fact that he has a mom who loves him. The love in return now seems limited to Mother's Day or my birthday. So that makes two times a year that I hear his voice. There are no face-to-face visits, only brief and mundane conversations about the weather. In fact, I have not seen him in person for years now. How heartbreaking this is for me, his mom. I doubt The Princess even cares and probably would rather he not call at all. As it is, he only calls from his car while driving home from work. During the pandemic, when he had to work from home, it was rare that we even spoke. It must be difficult to live with someone who controls your every move. I do not believe that is God's intent for the relationship between husband and wife. In the Bible, I find it rather interesting that the book of Proverbs speaks about the duties of wives. **Proverbs 27:15** says, *"A quarrelsome wife is like the dripping of a leaky roof in a rainstorm."* I take it somewhat literally that she "rains on his parade" if he tries to reach out to us.

Upon our return, my husband was assigned summer duty at the base. A few months later, I became pregnant again, and this time everything went well.

I went to the base clinic for all my checkups, where I was seen mostly by midwives. I may have seen a doctor only once or twice during the pregnancy. Being stationed at one of the largest Army bases in the country meant there were too many pregnant women for anyone to receive special treatment. When I went into labor for the first time, I truly believed it was the real thing. In the weeks leading up to it, my husband and I tried to do everything right, like most young and inexperienced couples who want to be fully prepared. We also knew my parents would not be able to come after the birth because they were elderly, and it would have been too exhausting for them to travel and help once we returned home. So, it was important for us to understand what to expect. We attended Lamaze classes and took Red Cross courses on how to care for babies. Still, nothing could have prepared us for what was about to happen.

I called my husband at work, and he came straight home as I had been timing my contractions and knew I was in labor. We got in the car and rushed to the base, which was about a 20-minute drive from our apartment. We went to the labor and delivery area and waited. When they finally examined me, they told us I was not in true labor and to go home. Seriously, I was sure I was in labor. There were just too many women having babies at this hospital on post. They just could not fit me in. Ugh. On the way home, my husband decided he needed to get food and stopped at Burger King. It is interesting how men always want to eat in crisis situations. To this day, I will not eat at Burger King. However, it was convenient to stop and go through the drive-thru as we returned home. He asked me if I wanted anything, and in my discomfort, and also in anger that they sent us home, I had him order me a big, juicy Whopper with everything on it and greasy fries. If you remember when you went into labor, one of the things they tell you is not to eat anything. Well, I went ahead and ate that whole burger with everything on it as I expressed my pain and discomfort to my poor husband. About two hours later, my contractions were much worse, and he called the base. They told us to return because I was probably in labor. Oh yes, I was definitely in labor.

At this point, I will tell you that husbands have no clue about the pain of childbirth, right? They think they know better than you. So, as I was in this horrible labor, trying to do the Lamaze breathing technique as we had practiced, and he was there as my coach, helping me breathe, I informed him that I needed something more for the pain.

Of course, his response was, "No, you can do this without any medication. It is healthier for the baby, and you can do this." At that moment, the Whopper came out of me with a force that felt like the pressure of a volcano erupting. Then I started shouting at him, and I think I said I hated him several times. I was very sorry later because I do love him. Finally, after nine hours of misery and being stuck in transition, they said I was ready for delivery and would be taken to the delivery room. At that moment, we heard a scream in the hallway. My husband went to the door to see what was going on. Another woman and her husband were standing in the hall with the baby about to come. They rushed her into the delivery room, where I was supposed to go, and we were put on hold. Eventually, they wheeled me to another labor room. That day, my little boy came into this world. Such joy. The miracle of birth. Our son is a true gift from God. He was perfect, and I was so thankful to God for giving me this miracle. My son, my one and only son, the boy who would grow up, become his own man, and marry "a princess."

Well, I thought it was all going great after delivery until I was wheeled into a ward of about 25 beds with only curtains around each bed to give privacy. Two hours after I delivered, I was told I had to go take a shower in a large bay of showers with just curtains for privacy. I do not know about you, but I am a very private person when it comes to personal matters, so I was extremely uncomfortable. Then I was told to walk down a very long corridor to a large cart where trays were stacked on a rack, and I was to get my breakfast. The trays were metal and felt like a ton of bricks being carried all the way back to that uncomfortably hard bed to eat. Seriously, did these military personnel not understand the situation? I had just gone through unbelievable pain to have a baby. Then they wanted to continue the discomfort. I was examined several times and checked by the nurses on duty. Then, within 24 hours, yes, that fast, I was released with our son and went home to our apartment.

This one is my precious son, whom I believed would be everything I had hoped and dreamed. As a mom, do you remember how you felt when you held your baby boy? You imagine giving him all the best things you did not have. Do you remember how the king and queen look over their beautiful baby in those fairy tales? Little did I know that someday my son, my little prince, would marry his "princess," but not the one from the movies I had imagined for him.

Life was interesting at that time. My husband was always working or going to school. He applied for an ROTC scholarship and was able to have his commanding officer, who later became a very well-known public figure, write a referral for him. He was accepted, and then we had to make some life choices. We had to find a place to live, and since he was going to school full time, we would be living on a very small fixed income. Yes, very little money to support his wife and new son. I look back with amazement at how God has always provided for us. **Isaiah 41:10** says, *"So do not fear, for I am with you; do not be dismayed, for I am your God. I will strengthen you and help you; I will uphold you with my righteous right hand."*

We were interviewed by a couple who had a very small house right next to the college. That would be perfect because I could have our car when needed to take our son to doctor appointments, get groceries, and run errands, and he could attend school by walking.

I was not working at the time, and our money was very tight. One night, my husband was helping out at a basketball game at the college, and he came home complaining of severe pain in his side. The landlady was so kind and took our baby boy to her home next door while I drove my husband to the hospital. They gave him an enema and told him it was just bad gas and to go home. It was a horrible night of pain, and seeing how the pain was increasing and he was hurting so badly, I drove him back to the hospital. They performed an emergency appendectomy and told me that it had almost ruptured, so we got him there just in time. Thank you, Lord, for that protection.

He recovered, but we were faced with hospital and doctor bills, so I had to find a job. God is always looking out for us, and I was able to get a job with a company that allowed me to work only a few hours in the office, and the rest of the time I could work at home and take care of our son. We were so thankful for that arrangement, as it gave me the ability to stay home and not have to pay extra for a sitter while my husband was attending classes. That June, he graduated with a BS degree and was commissioned as a second lieutenant in the U.S. Army.

Chapter 5
Life on the Move

Here we go again with another move and a new lifestyle. I had no idea what being an officer meant or what my husband would be doing, but I knew our lives were about to change again. Little did I know what was expected of me as an officer's wife, either. It meant going to teas and serving the general's wife and other high-ranking officers' wives, as I was just a lowly lieutenant's wife. I learned a lot during this time period about the ways of the military, at least for officers' wives. I admire all the people who serve our country, but I am especially proud of their supportive wives. Military life is not an easy one, and you basically have no life of your own because the military handles it all for you. It is hard on families when their husbands and fathers have to leave them for duty. It is even harder for those who have to serve overseas and can be gone for a year or more. I remember meeting some Navy wives during our time in the military. I was new to this life, and I was shocked when they told me their husbands were typically gone six to eight months at a time at sea. They had to be both father and mother to their children when their spouses were gone. So, I can say that the experience of being in the military did a lot of character building in both of us.

At this time, our son was just two. He was a bright little guy who spoke early, walked early, and was potty trained by two. Back then, mothers would potty train early. I know there is a different mindset about these things now, but it was great and a money saver not having to buy diapers anymore. I have to say that the best book ever at that time was "Potty Training in a Day." Of course, that is a book not found on library shelves anymore, but honestly, it really worked for both of my children. It was not exactly a day, but it certainly was quick, and it was amazing that the ideas really worked. Besides, our son was now much easier to travel with, and there was a lot less to pack, which was a good thing because we were on the move again.

My husband's assignment was in another state, so we were moved to a new location. Fortunately, we were in another southern state, to which by now I had become acclimated to the nice warm weather. My husband was assigned to the Reception Station.

That is the place where new recruits go through before they are assigned to their company, where they will train. We lived in a townhouse that we had found off post and began the new journey. I spent my time taking care of our son while my husband worked. We applied to move into on-post officers' quarters to help with our finances. He came home one day and said we were authorized to move, so we packed up again and moved into our townhouse living space on post. I have not mentioned this before, but at this point, I will share with you that I have had 32 kitchens in my 51 years of marriage. We are experts at packing and moving!

We really enjoyed living on post because we were all a community, and there were lots of children, so my son learned early about playing and sharing with others. When my son turned three, we enrolled him in a small preschool on post. It was only three days a week, but he absolutely loved it. He was writing his name and doing all kinds of fun activities. We had only one car, so one day my husband decided that if he had a motorcycle, he could take our son to school and I would be able to have the car for running errands, grocery shopping, and appointments.

Now, you may question that or maybe even be totally horrified that we would take our three-year-old son on a motorcycle anywhere. Please do not judge us. At the time, we were young and thought it was not an issue. He had his own helmet, and he held on tightly to his dad, and we all survived the experience. Would I suggest allowing your children or grandchildren to ride at that young age? I would say absolutely not. But it was a very short distance, and he was on a post where the speed limit was only 30 MPH. I also made a pact with my husband that our son would only ride the bike to and from school, and most of the time, I handled transportation in the car.

Speaking of cars, we were a family with one vehicle. If you have never moved as much as I have, you have no idea of the costs involved each time you have to uproot and relocate. It is a financial burden that continues for years. At that time, as a young officer's family, we were only able to have one car. It worked out fine for us, and I was able to use it whenever I needed to run errands or take our son to his pediatrician.

During our stay at this assignment, I became pregnant again but miscarried. It was devastating to have it happen again. Of course, the first thing you do is ask God, "Why?" Another miscarriage is so hard on a woman.

It is especially hard when you are surrounded by military families who all have lots of children. It seemed that each time I went to the PX to shop, I was surrounded by kids. In that state of mind, I seemed to notice all the pregnant women even more. I knew it was not their fault that I had lost another baby, but my mind was not very positive. If you have ever lost a child or experienced a miscarriage, you can understand that my mind and heart were in a dark place. I kept asking God why He allowed it to happen to me again. Perhaps this fetus was also deformed, and God was sparing me from something I just could not handle. In the future, I did experience one more miscarriage several years after the birth of our daughter. God was still in control, and we managed to get through the loss.

For whatever the reason, our sweet church members sent food, and our group leader came to talk with me and offer comfort and support. I love how being involved in a church brings loving people together to help others in times of need. Because we had to move often and were uprooted every few years, we always found a church home that provided a sense of security during the periods we lived in a particular area. I am so thankful to all those church families who always made us feel welcome and loved, even knowing that we were not permanent members and would eventually move on.

Before moving again, the Army decided my husband had an aptitude for computers, so they decided he should attend their special training school in Indiana for three months. Of course, it was not ideal for my son and me to live there temporarily while my husband would be attending classes and having homework all the time, so I decided that I would take my son and go back home to visit my parents and family and stay with them while he was away. It worked out well, as my parents were getting much older and could not travel much, so it was a perfect time for them to spend quality time with their grandson. I cherish those days of watching him grow and being around our family, as it became much harder later for us to have that time together.

After his training and getting back to his assignment, my husband decided to get his Master's Degree in Public Administration. He loved history and politics, so this was a good time for him to attend night school at the university in the city while working his military job during the day. It was a very hard time for us as a couple. I was always with our son, while he was either working, studying, or going to classes at night. It was not the best of times for us as a couple because of all the stress.

This was also a time of real bonding with my son because he was the center of my life at that time, and I spent most of my time focusing on him while my husband was busy working and going to school. In hindsight, I could have done a better job of supporting my husband, and we grew apart during this period. My heart was hurting, and my spiritual life was lacking. As a Christian, I always felt it was easy to be close to God, but sometimes that has been my weakness, and Satan loves to attack us when we are not living and breathing God's Word every day. It is so important to feed on His Word daily and make it a heart's desire to be more like Jesus. I had lost my focus on Him, and it was not a good time for either of us. All that said, we managed to get through that period in our lives, and I was very proud of my husband for trying to better himself for his family. He graduated from the university with honors and now has an MA in Public Administration.

Soon, my husband got orders to move us to another state on the East Coast to be assigned to the Recruiting Command. Before we left the housing quarters, we had to thoroughly clean the townhouse, also known as quarters, mostly done by me, with bleach and all kinds of strong chemicals in order to pass inspection. It was of utmost importance that we pass the inspection so we could move out. What I did not know at that time was that I was pregnant with our daughter. Maybe it was the pregnancy making me feel nauseous, but I am sure it was mostly the horrible smells coming from those cleaning products. I am so thankful to God that she was fine and I had no issues or complications related to those horrible smelling liquid cleaners. God protected her, the small miracle inside me, from having any mental or physical issues.

The assignment was in a beautiful, history filled city. We loved the beauty, especially in spring with the dogwoods and azaleas. We were able to buy our very first home, a cute one-story house with a little porch out in the suburbs. It was a new subdivision and right by the elementary school. So, I would walk my son to kindergarten every day, then wait for him and walk back to the house in the afternoon. It was not only a great time for us, but it was good exercise as well. How I walked through a small wooded area to get to the school while being very pregnant, I will never know.

I did not even think about the possibility of snakes, creeping critters, or stumbling and falling flat on my very pregnant stomach. How great is our God for His infinite protection and safety over us.

It was in May when our beautiful daughter was born. Thankfully, there were no military hospitals in the area when I had to deliver, so I was able to give birth in a civilian hospital. What a different experience compared to my 24-hour stay at the base hospital. Our daughter was perfect, beautiful, and adorable, and my husband got to spend a little time with her when she was first born. I think back then, he was only allowed one day off, and that was to bring us home from the hospital. I believe now dads can take "paternal leave" from their companies for up to six weeks. Wow, that would have been so nice for the extra help. Instead, my days were filled with taking care of her and our son. He was such a great big brother. Even though they are five years apart, during the early years, he was great at helping me. But five years is a big gap, and they were never really close due to the age difference. However, I believe they loved and respected each other until he married "the princess," who made it clear that it was only about her and her family, and his sister is no longer part of his life.

Chapter 6
Confusion

Life was going fine, and then the Army decided my husband should go to Atlanta for an assignment there. We had only owned our home for about six months at the time. I remember the financing rates were around 14.5 percent back then. We are so fortunate right now that rates are not that high. I wonder if we will ever see those numbers again. Surely, I hope not. No one was buying anything back then, including homes, unless it was absolutely necessary, because no one had extra money. I fear we are living in a time warp and returning to those days. Anyway, we had to find a buyer pretty quickly. Our real estate agent was great and found a veteran who would purchase it through a one-month rental purchase agreement and a VA loan. That was wonderful news for us. However, they wanted to take possession right away, so we only had a couple of weeks to move out. Oh, but wait, the Army decided to keep my husband in the current location. We were not moving after all.

So, I had to quickly find a rental house so we could enroll our son in first grade. Thankfully, this was all happening during the summer and not during the school year. Yes, I had to do this alone because my husband had to work. Government jobs are very different than jobs in the private sector. Unfortunately, what we could afford was not in the area where we were living, and with no rentals available there, I found a rental house in a nearby community but in a different school district. Our son was very good at adapting to new situations, so he started school while I cared for our baby. Then, in their infamous way, the Army decided my husband should go to the new location after all and transfer within a couple of weeks. Wait a minute. I had just moved our household and family to this house, sold our first real home, and now they wanted my husband to go to another state. Also, every time we moved, it added expenses to our fixed income. As a dutiful military wife, you learn to either accept it or part ways. So, I did what a military wife does and handled everything that needed to be done. Since our military days, I have always had the utmost respect for wives who are left to be mothers, fathers, taxi drivers, and everything else for their families. Within a month, my husband moved ahead of us. We wanted to be sure he was truly staying there, so for three months I lived in that rental house, three states away, alone with an eight-month old baby and a six year old. That meant taking my son to school and picking him up every day, caring for our baby daughter, managing the house, running errands, and doing everything by myself.

How different the world is today, as these princesses complain about all they have to do, yet they have husbands around who can help them out, or they have maid services, nannies, lawn crews, and you name it to provide them the time they need to run to the gym, eat out with their BFFs, and have their "me" time. I know it's a different time, but I guess having gone through all those years of being a single parent at times and doing so much by myself made me stronger and better able to cope with difficult situations. I am not comparing families of today with when I was a young mom, as I know it's a totally different world that I am living in now. I just wonder about the future and where we are headed, as people just don't seem to have the strength and ability to cope with hardships and challenging situations.

Finally, my husband was positively certain he was there to stay and told me to pack up because we were joining him. Yay. Now the fun really began. I learned one important lesson from this experience, and that is not to let your husband find you a place to live without you.

He found us a rental house in the area south of the post, where he could commute to work easily. He was told by the agent that it was a great family community. So, when we finally arrived to be with him, we walked into a dark, smelly house with gold and green floral wallpaper from the 1960s, orange shag carpeting that, in the light of day, was stained all over from who knows what, and a dark, all wood paneled family room. It was a split -level home with three bedrooms and one bath. The washer and dryer area was on the lower level, through the family room and out onto an enclosed patio. The refrigerator, which had been there when my husband viewed the house with the agent, had been stolen while the house was vacant, so the owner managed to find an old refrigerator to replace it. Yes, it matched everything because it was "harvest gold." I remember sitting down in a heap and crying about how bad it was and how I would have to disinfect the entire house before the children could sleep there safely. I pulled myself together and cleaned it thoroughly from top to bottom. Later, my husband shared with me that he had looked at that house when it was almost sunset, so it was quite dark inside. Not a good excuse. He still knows to this day how much I disliked that place. We lived there for about a year before we found a house to buy in the same community, but in a new development with a great elementary school.

During this time, my husband and I were concerned about military life, moving whenever we were told, and having no control over our lives, but we also wondered how it would affect our two children, being uprooted so often. There didn't seem to be any roots for growing a family, and it felt like we would always be moving. This is one of those God "funnies," as we continued to move many times over the years. My husband was contacted by an officer he had previously known. She had gotten out of the military and was working for a large company downtown, and they were looking for former military officers to work for them. So, we talked and prayed about it. He gave her his resume, was interviewed, and was hired. At that time, the salary offered was much higher than a military officer's pay, and the benefits far outshone what the government had offered him. Ten years is a good point to decide whether you are staying and retiring with the military or getting out to join the business world. We both felt it was the right decision for our family at that time.

Chapter 7
Adapting to Change

So, with added income, better benefits, and a new life ahead, we bought a house. House number two. We bought a cute two-story house with a small porch and a large backyard for the children. I enrolled our son in school, and we had a great neighborhood with lots of children his age. My husband stayed as an active-duty reservist and was promoted to captain and later became a major. We joined a church and grew to love the area. This big southern city was a great place to live, and our daughter developed a love for history like her dad. We lived in a community near the hometown featured in "Gone With The Wind." The Civil War hospital and a cemetery shaped like the state from an aerial view were located in the area. The home called "Tara" was not far from a drive for us, and the old train depot, where many soldiers once passed through, stood in the middle of the small town. So, it was a wonderful historical area for learning about the past.

My son had a wonderful elementary school education. A teacher once told me that she could see him becoming a president someday. He had a personality that everyone liked, and he was exceptionally bright and placed in the gifted and talented program. So, in second grade, he began his journey in the gifted program at school, which continued through his senior year. He loved the classes and was enriched by the experience, which later paid off when he went to college and secured a great job. I am not one of those "bragging" moms and never spoke about it to others, but I feel I can share this with you and hope you won't judge me. My daughter is equally bright, but they have different talents and are unique in their own special ways.

Soon, we discovered that we could use a bigger house, with our kids growing and needing more play space. We searched in the area and found a beautiful home on a cul-de-sac that was in the process of being built. We took our children over to look at it, and they thought it was great. The backyard was wooded with a small stream, which later, during a hurricane, flooded the house next to us, so we were very thankful we were on higher ground. This became one of my favorite houses, as it was that typical two-story colonial with blue shutters and a large colonial blue wooden door with a knocker, of course.

We were able to move into this pretty brick two-story home so that the kids could start school in the fall at new schools. The neighborhood had plenty of children, and my son started friendships that have lasted all his life. In fact, several of them were at his wedding party. There were five boys who played together and grew up to be teenagers, and a couple of them even went on to attend the same university. They were all in the same middle school at this time and found they had a lot in common. Soon, a really great relationship formed between him and another boy who lived down the street. We got to know the parents as well and formed a friendship that has also lasted all these years.

Our daughter was going to preschool and was heading off to kindergarten. A classmate's mom was a kindergarten teacher and asked me if I would want to go to work with my daughter. I thought it was a great time to work again, and I would be involved in school with both children. So, I became a licensed paraprofessional, which in the state allowed me to work with children who needed extra help and also assist teachers in the classroom. It was a great experience, and I worked at two schools during that time period. I worked for almost ten years in the school district and worked with some amazing teachers who I know touched many lives forever in a positive way.

Life was really going well for us at this time. The kids were happy, and my husband had moved to a new job with a large Fortune 500 company and was moving up the ladder of corporate success. The kids were doing very well in school. The middle school years were busy, as my son was not only active in sports, but he had also found a love for the gifted program called "Odyssey of the Mind." It is a world-renowned program that focuses on team building, problem solving, and creativity. He was placed on a team at school, and they were able to advance to local, state, and national competitions. He enjoyed the fun and the challenges of the program. Before long, my husband and I started getting involved as well. I coached a team from the elementary school with our daughter and also helped with a team at her school. My husband and I together became involved with coaching the high school students. As parents, we were always involved in some way with the schools, as we felt that was our way of knowing what was going on in our children's lives.

We soon became coaches for our son's team, which advanced from regional to state and then to World Finals in their senior year. They worked very hard together and, besides being classmates in the gifted program, they were also involved in sports, managed to keep their grades up, and remained at the top of their graduating class. The team won first place and took the trophy back to their school.

Right here, I would like to add a short story about how a friend's daughter-in-law treated her son's sister. This person's son was a good friend and wanted to share this incredible story. As the bridal party was getting ready, her daughter, who was basically ignored by the sisters and the entire wedding party, including the daughter-in-law's mother, overheard "The Princess" making fun of her brother and his best man about their enthusiasm for being creative and participating in what she called "stupid competitions." This did not leave a good impression on her daughter about the kind of girl her brother was marrying. To make fun of her soon-to-be husband seemed unbelievable. Oh, these princesses!

Chapter 8
Time Passes Fast

Many parents today are so wrapped up in their own lives that they do not seem to have time for their children and what is going on with them. I know this as a fact from teacher friends who share stories about the parents of their students. My husband and I were always of the mindset that even if I did not work a high-paying job, we could get by financially, even if it meant we were not driving luxury cars or having swimming pools in the backyard, so that I could always be there for our children. My job with the school system afforded me the opportunity to earn some money, but it also gave me the time to spend with our children. We always felt we should be available to them and support our children, but we also instilled in them the importance of being independent and not relying on us or anyone else to take care of them. My husband traveled around the world for his job and was sometimes gone three to four weeks at a time, but he always managed to be present for dance recitals, soccer games, and any events that involved our children. He coached soccer teams so he could spend more time with our son,

I took our daughter to dance classes, and we did all the driving around and attended school activities together. I feel like parents today do not have that same priority, and the family unit is in need of repair. This is a different world than when our children were growing up. Most people would agree that technology has defined our society, and not always for the good of our families.

So thus far, you can hopefully see that we moved a lot and had to overcome many obstacles. I guess our moving so many times also taught our son that he could live anywhere and do anything. He was placed in situations with our moves where he had to make friends and adjust, whether it was a new school, neighborhood, or sports team. Here again is where there was a definite difference in the way my son was brought up and the way his wife was brought up, as she never moved out of state or held a job outside her home state. He had to learn to adapt, but strangely, I think that is difficult for her.

The high school years went by fast, and, as you know, as a parent of a junior in high school, it meant trying to find a college. Being a bright student, he really wanted to attend a large university that could lead to a strong career path. We took him to visit several schools, but all the out-of-state schools were extremely expensive, and it was very hard seeing the disappointment on his face when we went to the finance office and learned that we simply could not afford them. I am sure you have been there before. Luckily, our state decided to put the Lottery in place, and one of the initiatives the governor included was that the funds would be used for education. Because of that program, our son was able to attend an amazing college that many bright students attend. His tuition was covered, and books were included, as long as he maintained a B average or above. That arrangement worked well for students until maintaining a B average became much more difficult. If an A student was ahead of his peers in high school, then college often changed everything when classes became much harder and more challenging and they would then lose the scholarship.

Chapter 9
Big Changes

So, there he was in his first year of college downtown, away from his home in the suburbs. He moved into campus housing for the first year, which was quite nice. We were having a normal life until my husband came home asking how we would feel about moving overseas. Mind you, our daughter was in middle school. She was as happy as a clam, involved in cheer dance, and loved her school, her friends, and everything about her life. My husband said they would fly us over to have a look and see. This was a huge decision for all of us, and it meant moving to a third world country halfway around the world.

The company flew us business class, which was wonderful for such a long flight. It was our daughter's first long flight, and being in business class at fourteen seemed pretty awesome. They then put us up in a luxury hotel, which was even more impressive. From that point of view, you would say that life could get very nice indeed. My husband seemed to think he could handle the workload, and when we returned home, we made the big decision after much prayer, seeking to know if it was truly God's will. I think our son was probably a bit upset that his family was moving that far away. However, the enticement was that the company would fly him overseas twice a year to see us, also in business class. A college freshman traveling overseas in business class certainly sounded appealing, right?

So, with everything packed and ready to go, our house was put on the market with the company's agency that handled this type of sale. One of the hardest things my husband had to do was sell his refurbished two-seater sports car. It was a very cute, British-made car and truly one of a kind in the area. It broke our hearts to give it up, but as we learn in life, it is not about possessions. Still, it was hard when the gentleman buyer and his son came and drove it down the street, with the top down, of course, and we knew it was no longer our car.

At this point, we took a road trip back north to see my parents and siblings, and then came back home to move during the Christmas break. Why is it that we always seem to move during the Christmas holiday?

Leaving our son behind was one of the hardest things I had ever done as a mom. It broke my heart that he had to stay, but we knew it was best for him and his future. His best friend's family in our neighborhood was kind enough to say they would keep an eye on him, and it helped that he and several others from his close group of high school friends were also attending the same college. Also, we would have summers to spend back home, so that seemed to ease my worried mommy mind.

We decided to make the trip over to Asia memorable, so we stopped at a few places along the way. Our first stop was San Francisco, where we spent a day taking our daughter to special and memorable places. She loved the museums and Fisherman's Wharf. Her first visit to California was truly amazing to her. But the next stop was even better, Hong Kong. What a wonderful place filled with rich culture, beautiful sightseeing, ferry boat rides, and viewing the city from the waterfront at night with a million lights twinkling like stars. Hong Kong was a place that stole my heart. I fell in love with that city and was able to experience it both before the turnover to China and afterwards. It is very interesting how it changed after China assumed control, as it somehow lost some of its unique personality and charm. I still, to this day, list it as one of my favorite cities in the world. While living in the Philippines, Hong Kong became one of our favorite getaway destinations. I remember going for weekends just to shop, enjoy delicious food, and soak in the vibrant atmosphere. It was especially fun when three other ladies I had met joined me for an all-girls weekend in Hong Kong. The weekend was wonderful as we walked through the open markets, bartering for "knock-offs" like Gucci, Fendi, and other famous designer brands.

We ate at a Chinese restaurant that served an amazing lunch. We went everywhere in taxis and never felt in danger. We visited the night markets, which were even more exciting with the exotic smells of food cooking, people of all cultures walking around, different languages being spoken, and browsing the amazing items that were for sale. There were some items that I was not so sure about, such as a goat's head with its eyes staring at me while it cooked over an open pit. It did nothing for my appetite. However, the jewelry and scarves were beautiful. To this day, I regret not buying a lovely coral necklace that would have been so fun to wear. It was an amazing weekend until we returned. My husband and I were getting closer to our departure from the Philippines, and apparently, there was something about my visa that I did not understand, and we were unaware of it when I took the trip.

We were all going through customs, and the three ladies in front of me went through with no issues. Then, when I handed the officer my papers, he told me I could not proceed, and I was escorted to a room where a large man questioned me about why I was returning to the Philippines. As I was being escorted away, the other ladies looked at me with apprehension and worry, unsure of what was happening. I can still remember the fear on their faces for me. I tried to call my husband at work and, of course, I could not reach him. Isn't that always the way when you urgently need to contact your husband, and he is not answering? For half an hour, I kept trying to reach him while the officer repeatedly told me I would have to buy a ticket and return to Hong Kong. I kept insisting, "No, I live here in the Philippines!" At that point, I was truly frightened. Then he asked me a strange question about whether I had a ticket, and I told him that, as a matter of fact, I had two tickets in my passport folder to return to Hong Kong because my husband and I had decided we wanted to visit one last time before going back to the States. Suddenly, he told me I could go and escorted me out the door. I left that area as quickly as I could and found the ladies waiting for me, anxious to know exactly what had happened. I can tell you that I felt extremely uncomfortable and truly panicked. Did I pray? Absolutely.

Chapter 10
Life As An Expat

Moving to a third world country seemed fine when you lived in a luxury hotel for three months. We had a car and a chauffeur (a driver, as they were called, but someone who could handle the crazy traffic that caused me fear just watching it), and our daughter was taken to the International School every day by him. He was responsible for picking her up as well. His duties included taking my husband to and from work and driving me wherever I needed to go, and if we decided to travel or needed to go to the airport, he was responsible for our transportation. I basically did not drive a car for three years, except during our visits home. Looking back, there are some days now when I would love that luxury with our crazy drivers and traffic. My family is always teasing me that I would be a "Driving Miss Daisy" kind of person. I also miss that luxury of having a door opened and closed for me all the time. I guess there were some nice benefits to living in a third world country.

We lived on gourmet food with no cooking or cleaning at all, so you can imagine the rich food we were eating and the lack of exercise we were getting. Basically, living the life of luxury was, perhaps, not as great as it sounds.

I still remember that as we were leaving the hotel to move into the house the company provided, one of the doormen, whom we had come to know by name, looked at me and said, "Oh, mum, you have gotten so fat!" Oh yes, I knew my clothes were tighter, and I really did not need to hear that from anyone at that time, as I was already feeling badly. However, I have to say that living there gave us insight into the culture of the Philippines. We found the people to be loving, family-oriented, crafty, musical, and at times very childlike in their behavior and thinking. So, I decided I would not hold it against him, as he probably did not mean it to be hurtful, but it still hurt.

Then we moved into our gated, one- story house in a prestigious neighborhood where there were literally mansions. Due to my husband's position with the company, we were given only a very limited number of choices, and the one we chose was by far one of the smallest. We decided that we would be much more comfortable in a smaller house. However, we had expat friends who were truly living in mansions with many rooms, and they all needed maids. The house we finally moved into had shiny dark green tiles decorating the front, and we eventually named it "Green Acres" after the Green Acres. Partly it was because the wiring, which was 220V, looked ancient. In fact, here is a little history of my first attempt to plug in my brand -new bread machine that I brought with me from the States. Of course, the machine used our voltage of 120V, but the outlets in this house were wired for both. I was so excited about using my new machine because we found the bread in this country was very sweet, and the texture was something we could not get used to, so this was going to be my solution to that issue. I had barely touched the outlet plug and thought I was heading for the 120V slot, but accidentally grazed the 220V and BOOM! I literally fried the machine. I was not happy at all. But it truly scared me to death when it happened. Our stove was gas, which was supplied from a propane tank in the attic. There was a small tube that ran down the back wall behind the stove that served as the gas supply line. Oh yes, it was scary indeed, especially when we smelled gas one day and found out there was a leak up in the attic. The entire attic was filled with fumes, and the poor man who served as our guard had to climb up and then call someone from the company's handymen to come fix it.

We also had something that many houses did not have: a generator. We were very blessed to have a generator that could run everything in the house when the power went out, which it did quite often, especially during the dreaded "rainy season," which always meant typhoons.

The company was generous to provide us with a new stove, refrigerator, and washer and dryer that were more "American" so we could use them and make the transition a bit easier. However, being a tropical country, everything outside became rusty or mildewed. I was never quite sure how clean our clothes were since the washer and dryer were located outside on the covered patio. This was also the area where there was a wooden table with chairs, where our guard and anyone working around the house would stop and eat their lunches. There was also a dark, dingy room outside for maids to stay if you chose that arrangement. They used this covered open area for cooking, including the use of a rice cooker. Rice is a main staple in this culture. It was often smelly from the fish, rice, and whatever else they cooked and ate. That smell lingered right near the washer and dryer, so I sometimes imagined going places and worrying that I smelled like cooked fish.

Another interesting fact is that the people are very superstitious. When our first maid worked for us, she refused to stay in that small room. Eventually, our guard told us that a maid had died there, or at least that was the rumor about the room, so no one wanted to sleep in that tiny space. There were still a bed and a cabinet for clothing, and we knew the guard occasionally took naps there, and probably the lawn care worker did as well. Speaking of this man, he somehow managed to borrow my husband's American made tools that he had brought along. One day, my husband was searching for one of his tools and noticed that not only that one but several others were missing. The guard explained to my husband that the yard worker had decided they were nice and would "borrow them" to use at his other jobs. Oh my. We learned from that incident that they felt it was acceptable to borrow without asking, and their philosophy seemed to be that what was yours was also theirs.

Most of the expats, especially those living in houses, had maids. I am one of those people who was brought up to do my own work, including housecleaning.

However, I learned very quickly that due to the horrible black air pollution, everything had to be cleaned every day. I remember when our things finally arrived from the States. Most of our furniture had been put in storage, including our piano, which had water damage when we finally moved back. As I was unpacking boxes, I thought it was going to be like living in the movie "South Pacific." The beauty of the islands, the sea breeze blowing in, the beautiful palm trees swaying, and the air is clean and pure. Ha, ha, on me, and back to reality. To this day, I am sure that someday we will all be diagnosed with a lung disease from the air pollution.

Anyways, I could not bring myself to have live -in help. We are very private people, and we were told that many of the hired helpers stole from the expats or played the "sympathy" card and were always asking for handouts even when they were paid well. We went through three maids before we found one who was sweet, trustworthy, and did not keep asking us for money. She was a believer and had the sweetest spirit. We did not mind helping her any way we could. It was sad to have to say goodbye to her.

We also went through a couple of drivers. They worked for the company, so they had attitudes, especially when it came to the families they were assigned to. If you were a VP or higher, they wanted that family. It became quite apparent that my husband was not a VP, so our driver decided to move to a new expat family where the employee was a VP. The next driver was not reliable and caused a lot of frustration. It became so frustrating that one day my husband just "lost it," made him pull over, got behind the wheel in downtown traffic, and literally drove up onto the sidewalk to get around traffic and the crowds of people because my daughter was late for school and he was late for work. People were fleeing as everyone tried to get out of the way of this crazy American. I was in the back seat, getting as low as I could, hoping that no one saw me with the crazy driver. After that, the driver was let go, and we finally got a sweet older gentleman who served us well until we left. He was quiet, a true gentleman who always opened the doors for us and carried our things into the house. He was truly one of the kindest people we met, and it was very sad when we had to say goodbye to him as well.

The International School was interesting. Our daughter attended there for 9th, 10th, and 11th grades. Only 25 percent of the students were Americans.

The rest of the school population was made up of wealthy local families, as well as students from Indian, Australian, Korean, and other Asian backgrounds. It was a wonderful experience for any child, as the school ranked high on the spectrum of education. Several of her instructors were from Ivy League schools, and the students were required to complete community service projects, which sometimes took her to places she would never have otherwise gone. It was a mixture of cultures, and it was great seeing her develop relationships with these other kids. She invited them over to our house and had swim parties. At times, she seemed to us like she had adjusted well, but at other times, we knew she hated us for taking her away from her perfect life back in the States. Now that she is older, she has told us that we were indeed right. One time, she even went as far as trying to make reservations to fly home. She was disappointed when she realized she had no money and no place to go since her brother was living on campus at the university.

During this time, as expats, there was a life that no one could understand unless they had lived as an expat in another country. There were times when it was very difficult to understand why God had placed us there. There was constant pressure on my husband to perform, which was especially difficult while working with people from many different countries. Working alongside the nationals was even harder. They did things differently, and in general, it was a huge adjustment for my husband. I could not fully relate to what he was going through because I was living a life without work, being chauffeured everywhere and enjoying outings, lunches, and coffee with friends I had made there. We even had a Starbucks in our neighborhood area, and I had my first frappuccino at that location. I regret now that I could have been more supportive and more understanding of what my husband was going through.

I am a very private person and rather introverted, especially in large groups of people. However, I joined the International Women's Club to meet people from different places. It was there that I became connected with the International Bible Study Group. That was where God truly showed me how I could love others from different countries, and I learned that they, too, went through many adjustments like we did. It was very meaningful to be able to sit down, pray with others, and feel God's presence.

They were all lovely ladies from everywhere: Australia, Singapore, Japan, New Zealand, and many different areas of the United States. I am grateful to this day for the love and support shown by those wonderful ladies.

During this time, I also developed friendships with several ladies whom I still keep in touch with even after all these years. One of these ladies was a beautiful woman from California. She and her husband were there with an oil and gas company, and there were quite a few families connected to that industry. She was the daughter of a Mexican field worker, and she knew how to cook authentic Mexican food. It was she who taught me how to make homemade flour tortillas, rice, and beans that my kids loved whenever I made them, because the recipes were so delicious. She was also gifted in arts and crafts and could create beauty from simple materials and pieces of artwork. She had joined the Garden Club and asked me if

I was interested in joining as well. I love flower arranging, as I had taken a course in flower design when my son was young.

We had so much fun learning from these very wealthy women about flower arranging, and we toured beautiful mansions to see their gardens. The highlight of the club was a large charity event where my friend made beautiful Christmas trees. She asked me to help her, and I thought it would be great fun. As I was watching her, I noticed her tree limbs were all going downward. I was making mine go upward like a blue spruce or pine tree that I was familiar with from the East Coast. She gently corrected me and explained that the tree limbs were supposed to go downward. "Strange," I thought. Then I realized she had never been outside of California, and many trees on the West Coast naturally droop downward. So all the trees were decorated with the limbs facing downward, as I learned.

To celebrate the event, we all dressed up. Little did I know that the Vice President of the country and several other national officials would be attending that evening. The Vice President of the Philippines was lovely and seemed very friendly and down to earth. We actually sat at a table right next to hers, which became a treasured memory of that evening.

Thinking back on some of those special events, it makes the difficult times seem less overwhelming in the bigger picture of life. I would never have visited an ambassador's residence in another country, become acquainted with his wife, or gone on outings with her. Nor would we have experienced many other things that normally would not have happened if we had stayed in the United States and never gone overseas.

I think experiences like these are great memories, but I really haven't shared them with many people over the years, because they don't understand what I went through and can't relate. But I keep those fond memories tucked away. If, however, you are or have been an expat and have had some of these experiences, then you can absolutely relate to them, and maybe they will bring back some of your more positive experiences. Being an expat is certainly not the easiest life.

Chapter 11
Reflections

At this point, I want to reflect on my son. He has never come out and said that he resented us leaving him to move overseas, but I think he has held ill feelings toward us that have never been voiced. Sometimes, as parents, you think you are doing the right thing and feel like God is moving you toward a place, but then, looking back, you wonder. He had a wonderful time visiting us and especially loved the travel to and from halfway around the world. He also got to see places that none of his friends would probably ever see. The two times a year he could come visit, we always planned it around his breaks, and we went to a new country each time. We spent Christmas in Australia, where we stayed in a hotel that overlooked Sydney Harbour with a view of the Sydney Opera House. We went to Christmas Beach on Christmas Day in Australia, for Pete's sake. How cool is that? Our family spent three weeks traveling together, going from Sydney, then to the Gold Coast and the city of Brisbane, and then up to the Great Barrier Reef.

While I am writing this, I have to stop and thank God again for His travel protection. On the day we were going on a dive boat, in The Great Barrier Reef, both my husband, son, and daughter were certified divers, it was gloomy and rainy. We heard there was some bad weather coming, but we did not realize, being there as travelers, that it was truly severe weather. In fact, they call it a "typhoon" in that area of the world, but the company we hired said they were still going out. So we packed ourselves up and met at the dock. We noticed there were no other boats going out, which should have alerted us, but when you reserve with a company in the area, you assume they know what they are doing. There was a large scuba diving company called Quick Silver that did go out, but later we found out they turned right back in, choosing to be cautious about the approaching weather.

But this dive boat we were on kept on going and was headed for the edge of the Great Barrier Reef. There were approximately 20 people, including crew, on this dive boat. The waves were getting bigger, and it was raining, foggy, and windy. They put down anchor at a spot, and the people who wanted to dive went in. We noticed that something just did not feel right. My son, daughter, and I stayed on the boat and just watched. Other people were starting to notice that no one was out there but us. When the divers came up, there was a problem. Apparently, the anchor rope had tangled around the propeller. Not good! Finally, a few of the crew master divers dove under and untangled it. We noticed people were starting to feel uneasy as the storms were rolling over us and the dive boat was being tossed around by the waves. The second stop was close to the edge of the barrier reef. My husband went down again with the other divers, and he told me that when you are under the surface of the water, you do not see or feel the storm. My kids wanted to see something as we were at the Great Barrier Reef! So, the diver masters said the rest of us could just snorkel. We went into the water, and it was impossible to see anything underwater due to the huge waves. I panicked when I looked around, and the waves were blocking my sight of my children, and I just wanted to get us out and back on the boat, when suddenly I felt a stinging sensation. The diver master yelled, "Blue bottles, get out of the water!" It was an order taken seriously, as we all tried to get back to the boat and get out of the water. People were shouting that they were being stung, and we had a difficult time just trying to swim back to the boat. One person was stung so badly that they had to be treated. Luckily, none of us had a reaction to the stings. As I was standing and watching for the divers, a gentleman looked at me and said, "Do you think we are drifting closer to the reef?" I noticed we had moved farther out. The storms had moved out, and it was not raining, but it was still cloudy. My concern for my children and husband was beginning to make me feel very uncomfortable. At this point, we were so ready for the boat company to take us back. Finally, the divers came up, and I was so glad to see my husband safely back. Unfortunately, the waves caused several people to get seasick, and no one wanted to eat the lunch the crew had prepared. We were sitting up on the upper part of the boat, where there were benches, and it was also the area where the captain was at the wheel. As the water was getting more and more turbulent and it was starting to get foggy as well, we noticed the captain was disturbed.

As we watched him, my husband leaned over and whispered in my ear that he could not see his buoy markers; he was lost. I sat there and just started praying intensely. We were over 30 miles out from shore, and all I wanted was to see land again. I was concerned for our lives, and I was trying to remain calm for my children, who did not know what was going on, except that they were thinking maybe this was not the best idea to be out on a day like this. Finally, after many hours, much later than when we were supposed to have returned, the boat came to the dock, and we were never so happy to be alive and safely back on land than at that moment.

So, interestingly enough, about a year later, we were watching the news, and this same dive company was seized for losing two divers at sea. The captain, who was the same captain we had, was arrested and put into prison. Later, a movie was made about these two divers who were lost at sea, and it was called "Deep Waters." You may have seen it, but it gave us chills thinking that this was the same company that had made really bad choices, taking us out that day. So, yes, we have all been to the Great Barrier Reef, but we had no sunshine and no pictures to share of this place that is known for its outstanding coral reefs, amazing fish and sea life, and as a great place to dive. Yes, I am sure it is, except when there is a typhoon!

My son came back on other breaks, and we were so fortunate to have gone to Tokyo right at the peak of the cherry blossoms in April. Oh, I cannot even begin to describe the beauty, the fragrance, the gorgeous trees all in shades of pink. It was so beautiful to see all the Japanese people, some dressed in traditional clothing, walking around the park. We visited a great museum that displayed samurai warrior gear and gorgeous artwork from Japan. We also took a tour to Mt. Fuji, which was cold and snow-covered, and we rode a tram up the side of a mountain. By the way, I am very fearful of heights, and I was terrified to go, but I so wanted to see everything from that view, so I went along and prayed the whole way. We took a bullet train back to Tokyo, which was the most amazing train ride ever. We almost did not make it, as our tour bus was late arriving, and we all literally had to run through the terminal to get on the train before it left. Fortunately, I was younger and in better shape. It was on this trip that we toured around Tokyo, which is a wonderful city with interesting sights and sounds. Even though I have the fear of heights, I managed to go to the top of Tokyo Tower, which gave us an amazing of view of all Tokyo.

It's also a very safe city. We went to the section of the city known for its electronics. At the time, it was the place to get all the latest and greatest in electronic games, as they were just becoming a huge fad. We rode the underground train system, which is efficient, extremely crowded, and almost impossible to navigate if you cannot read Japanese. Some kind young girl saw us and offered her help, which we really appreciated. When we got to our stop, of course, my son found a few things he really wanted to take back to college with him. He was like a little kid in a candy shop for the first time. We also discovered that we had left our passports at the hotel and had not thought that we would need them to pay with our credit cards. So, we left our two children there, and my husband and I jumped on the train to take us back to the hotel. We got the passports and jumped on the train to go back. We were only gone for probably an hour, and I never felt worried or concerned for their safety. I remembered one of the expats I knew, who had lived in Tokyo for several years and had one of her children delivered there, telling me that it was a perfectly safe place for her kids to go anywhere and not worry about them. Having that in the back of my mind helped me make the decision to leave my kids there.

We also went to Malaysia one time and stayed at a lovely resort. This was fine except that upon the day of arrival, some incident had happened that caused Americans traveling to be on alert. So, we did not venture out too much on our own, but stayed at the resort and only did one tour, which was on a bus. That was an interesting trip, as they stopped to show us cinnamon that was being harvested and laid out on large cloths in the middle of the road to dry. We saw a few monkeys swinging from trees and crossing the roads, and saw lemongrass growing. The tour guide was great with his explanations, and his English was perfect, which made the experience even more enjoyable.

On another trip, we went to Thailand. Bangkok is rich in history and traditions. We took a tour by bus up to the ancient city of Ayutthaya, which was the capital of the Burmese Empire. There were monks all over, walking around with their shaved heads and gold-colored robes. We were able to see elephants and other interesting animals along the way. My children were getting to do something most kids would never have experienced, and yet they were there with us, sharing in these moments and learning from each experience as well.

I wonder sometimes if my son appreciated these special trips. At one time, before marriage, I think he did appreciate all the experiences we tried to give to him, but all changed when he married "The Princess."

The return trip to Bangkok was by boat, which was fascinating, as we saw small wooden structures built into the water that were homes. We saw the long boats with motors, which you will remember seeing in a James Bond movie. We loved the food until we were at a dinner show. The girls were doing the traditional dance in their beautifully colored silk outfits as we were being served some delicious Thai food. Just before we got our coconut soup, my husband said something about not eating the green pepper in the soup, as it is so hot it will burn forever. It is known to be one of the hottest peppers in the world. I was enjoying the delicious smells of the soup, and the taste was unbelievably good. Then, what I thought was really a piece of a green bean was actually a piece of the chili pepper. Upon entering my mouth, I felt the burn all the way down to my stomach. I turned red as a tomato and was completely on fire! My husband took immediate action and told me to just eat the white rice to calm it, and I drank and drank water, including everyone else's at the table, before I finally was no longer burning. Lesson learned: do not eat anything green in the coconut Thai soup.

Chapter 12
Overseas Life

Living in another part of the world teaches you many things. God has made a beautiful world, and He just wants us to experience as much of it as we can. God also gave us different cultures so that we can learn, make friends, and appreciate others for their knowledge and skills. I am so thankful that we were able to have so many chances to travel, and that our son was able to share in these experiences that helped form him into a man who was experienced in appreciating other cultures. I am sure it has helped him with his job and in dealing with people who may be under his supervision in his work.

I must admit that there were many times I was lonely and missed my son and our home back in the States. When you are an expat, you have a completely different lifestyle. We were given many opportunities to share our ideas with other cultures, to learn from the country we lived in, and to understand how and why they do things the way they do.

But we were still foreigners and were sometimes treated as such. I had some not so pleasant experiences as an expat. I remember going to a store, and the person working behind the counter managed to keep me waiting while they helped everyone else who was a native. I remember seeing people living in tin sheet metal huts with dirt floors, yet they had TVs and microwaves! I remember riding in the car through back streets, where moms were bathing their babies in little basins outside their front doors, pouring water over them with a cup to rinse off the soap. I went with a few friends to a well-known shopping area where all kinds of crafting materials were sold very inexpensively. I was told not to bring a purse or anything that could be stolen, as it was a known area for thieves, but the goods sold were exceptionally cheap. I am a crafter, so I was happy to go along with my friends, and we had a local who was a friend of one of the ladies who knew what to do and how to get the best prices. Living in Asia, I learned to "barter" very well. My husband says I have made sellers cry as I got them down to a price I was willing to pay. One of the things I learned living overseas was to barter, and I became quite good at it. All was going well until the girl who was our guide noticed that she herself had her wallet stolen. I guess they did not really care that she was one of their own. I guess that shows how Satan is no respecter of persons and that sin is sin everywhere. Stealing is one of those things that is definitely evil. So, we had some good experiences living overseas, but we also had some experiences that really tested our faith. Life was certainly not without excitement, living in a third world country. We also had some amazing experiences that I will remember fondly. We visited the ambassador's home several times, and I was in the International Women's Club and got to go places and do things through that group. My favorite group was the International Women's Bible Study Group. They were a group of ladies from many different countries and even faiths, but we all served one God, loved each other, and supported one another. I still have a wonderful book given to me by a lovely Australian lady who had gone through some really tough times. Her husband's business had failed, and they moved their family to this country to start again. She and I prayed together and lifted each other up to the Lord. I will always remember these special moments and cherish the friendships that I made over there.

If you remember, we left our house back in the States with a real estate company provided by my husband's company to sell. At that time, we did not really know how long we would live overseas, so we thought it was in our best interest to sell. Finally, after several months, the agent managed to sell our beautiful house on the cul-de-sac to a family that was going to "rent" with an option to buy, as she said she could not find a buyer. I am not sure to this day why she could not find a buyer, as we would have come down on the price if she had given us some offers to consider. It also became apparent from what followed that she never checked on the house while it was sitting there empty or even after the people moved in to rent. I question her decisions for us, as apparently, the family that moved in were not reputable people. There were several children, and the neighbors said they did not think they even went to school. They had many animals in the house, even though the contract clearly stated that no animals were allowed, and the neighbors questioned their ethics and behavior. About three months after they were in the house, the real estate agent called me one day and said the people could no longer pay the rent and had apparently "skipped out," owing us money. We later found out they did not pay the utilities either. We were also told that our sweet neighbors on the cul-de-sac were all about to sell their houses because the situation had become that bad. We felt terrible for them, but we were also so upset that the agent had even placed people into the house, knowing they did not qualify for a loan.

Our son, being at the university there in the city, was the closest to the house. The rest of our family lived farther north, so they could not help us. Here we were, halfway around the world, unable to see what had happened with our own eyes. So, our poor son drove down to see the house. He called me literally in tears, saying the house was trashed. He said it was so awful he could hardly stand it. We told him to make sure it was locked, and I explained that I would be home with our daughter in another month, at the end of the school term, and that we would be back for the summer break. My husband could not get away from his project, so it was just my daughter and me making the trip. We flew home on the first of June and stayed in a hotel for the night upon arrival before we drove to the house the next morning.

I cannot begin to explain the feelings I had as I looked at my once beautiful two-story colonial house when we pulled up in the rental car. It reminded me of a haunted house, like the one on the TV show "The Munsters."

The once beautifully kept lawn, which my husband worked on so hard and which was his pride and joy, was dead, with weeds taller than a foot and the shrubs half dead. My daughter was in tears, but we did not even know the full extent of the damage yet.

When we pulled up and opened the garage door, there were roller skate or perhaps skateboard marks all over the once clean garage floor. We stepped up into the kitchen, which was so disgusting that I had to have a company haul the appliances away. There was a large hole in the sheetrock at the oak railing wall leading upstairs. There were marks all over the floor from kids possibly roller skating, as if it were a rink instead of a home. The once beautiful family room, with its beautifully built-in fireplace and bookshelves, was just as bad. There were stains on the carpet, and the ceiling fan was hanging halfway off, as if someone had pulled on it deliberately. Every room had some sort of damage, and you could tell the people were in a big hurry to move out because they left trash everywhere. But the one room that absolutely broke my heart was when my sweet daughter saw her bedroom. These people had birds in that room, apparently, as there was literally bird poop droppings all over the walls, the closet doors, the windows, everywhere there was poop, A whole mess. Even a few feathers were left behind as evidence.

As a mom, you never want your children to have to experience seeing this kind of damage done by people who abused and took advantage of us. But I felt horrible that my son was left alone to see this mess, which was his "home" for most of his growing years as well. My heart hurt that he was alone to bear witness to these damages first.

So that summer, I spent the majority of those months redoing the whole house. My kids and I painted, wallpapered, cleaned, and disinfected everything from top to bottom. I had new appliances brought in and new window treatments installed to replace the damaged ones. I had to hire people to come fix the landscape and lawn, and to continue to take care of the outside. What a way to spend a summer. I felt so bad for my kids having to deal with the mess. My husband was finally able to get away for a week to bring us back so our daughter could return to school. He never had to witness the extent of the damage done. Lucky him!

Unfortunately, we also had a big decision to make regarding the house that we still owned.

Our son was going to have to move back in for a period of time to keep an eye on it and commute to school. I guess these kinds of experiences help us to grow and help us deal with what life throws at us. He knew that it was not going to be easy or fun, but he understood that he was helping his family. I loved that he did that for us. Not many college-age kids would step up and leave their fun college life, but our son did that for us, and I was so proud of him.

Chapter 13
Going Home

Life went along, and we were miserable living away from the States. Our daughter was not happy, and I could see that the job was taking a toll on my husband, as it was so demanding. Having to deal with another culture and their ways was extremely difficult. We met people who loved that kind of life and were perfectly happy raising their children in international schools while moving every two to three years, but it was just not for us.

Our daughter was going to finish up her sophomore year of high school, and we decided that expat life was just not what we wanted. My husband was finishing up with the project, and we decided to move back so he could return to corporate life.

The week before we were to move back to the States, my husband received a letter from the U.S. Government, Department of Defense, informing him that because he was not able to complete his required training, he had even tried to do duty at the Embassy, but the Army said no, he was being honorably discharged. He was taken by surprise receiving this news. He had several good years of active and inactive reserve service and had hoped that when he returned to the States, he could continue his training. However, the Department of Defense had other ideas. With that news, even though he was close to retirement, but not close enough, he has never received any of the usual retiree VA benefits that a serving military officer would normally receive. To this day, I have harbored feelings of resentment that our government would do that, and I have had to work on that feeling and ask God to help me, especially knowing he could not receive any benefits that would help us in our later years. As a result, he was never able to receive a pension like many of his friends.

The company was always generous to its employees overseas. We had a life that most people cannot relate to, having never experienced it. We were moved into the Peninsula Hotel, which is a high-end luxury hotel. Can you imagine us walking into this luxury lobby with our little toy poodle accompanying us? They were fine with us bringing our little dog to the hotel and actually staying in our extremely nice room. I sometimes laugh thinking about our little "high society" poodle! It was very generous of the company to allow us to stay in a place so luxurious. We would never have experienced it if it had been paid from our own pockets!

The night before we were to leave, our friends gave us a wonderful farewell party at their condo. They had invited mutual friends, but they also had a special friend they had met during their expat moves. He was a former KGB agent who was now working a normal job and had traveled to visit his good friends. He was an interesting twist to our farewell party, and we found him fascinating as we listened to some of his stories in his broken English. Being so late getting back to our hotel, we decided we would just try to rest before the driver arrived at 5 AM to pick us up. Around 4:45, our phone rang, and our daughter was on the other end from her room. She wanted to know if we had some article of clothing or something to that effect. I really don't remember exactly, except the panic that we only had fifteen minutes to get ready and be downstairs for the car. We had no intention of falling asleep, but we did, and then we moved as fast as we could. We were absolutely certain we were not going to miss our flight, as our minds were set to leave and we were anxious to get home. To this day, my daughter teases me about how that was the fastest makeup job I had ever done! We made it to the airport in time after being dropped off by our Mercedes limo, didn't we arrive in style? We went to the international concourse and waited for that jumbo jet to take us on our twenty-two-hour trip back to the U.S.

Have you ever taken a pet on a plane? Our little toy poodle was in a small carry-on bag, so we could have him with us. The first leg was to Japan, and then we transferred onto a large jumbo jet for the trip to the States. When we got to our seats on the second level of this big plane, the flight attendant, who noticed we had a dog, informed us that we could not sit in our seats with him.

Why, I have no idea, because we had just traveled with him in those same seats to Japan. My husband was able to stay in his aisle seat in the front, but my daughter and I were escorted to the back seats for the trip to Detroit before taking the last plane to the East Coast and home. Apparently, this one particular flight attendant did not like pets, because the rest of the crew were so sweet. They were always asking about the dog or petting him. I even took him out of his bag and put him on my lap with a blanket over him, leaving only his little head exposed. Even the captain came by and gave him a little pat on the head, which I thought was so kind and thoughtful.

We arrived during summer break and had time to reflect on our future. My husband returned to his corporate offices downtown, but he quickly found out that he was no longer wanted or needed in the position he had held before we moved overseas. Instead of the beautiful office he had enjoyed, he was assigned to a cubicle to work. In addition, we had to attend mandatory repatriate classes designed to help us re-immerse ourselves into American culture. You might find it strange that this was necessary after only a few years abroad, but we quickly realized that everything had changed, and readjusting was far more complicated than we had anticipated.

We began to see life from a different perspective. Our daughter remarked that her peers seemed narrow-minded and clueless about the world beyond the United States. Her old friends, whom she had grown up with before we moved, had moved on and developed new relationships, leaving her feeling somewhat disconnected. We, as parents, also found it more difficult to make friends, as our interests and experiences no longer aligned with those of people we knew before. Our son had matured into a young man with his own set of values and goals, and coming back to the U.S. was not as easy or seamless as we had imagined.

Our home was no longer the same, either. Every time I walked through the rooms, I was reminded of the damage and heartache that had been hidden behind the new paint and wallpaper. Thoughts of what had been lost when we moved overseas weighed heavily on me. It was at this point that we made the decision to sell our house and start fresh in a new home. After searching, we found the house of my dreams and put in an offer. The owners accepted, but they were not willing to move until October. Meanwhile, we had a buyer ready for our current house who needed to move in immediately, leaving us in a challenging situation.

Sometimes, I would just sit and ask myself, "Why, God?" While my husband was busy at work, I took on the task of finding an apartment complex that would offer a short-term lease. Do you know how nearly impossible that is? Most complexes were unwilling to accommodate someone for just a few months, and it felt incredibly frustrating and stressful.

Finally, I found one willing to work with us, and we moved into a three-bedroom apartment while some of our belongings were still in a container being shipped to the U.S. from overseas. We were able to retrieve our stored items and move them into the apartment, which quickly became very full. Even in that crowded space, I felt a sense of relief knowing that we were slowly piecing our lives back together and beginning this new chapter, even if it came with challenges and uncertainty.

Then I had to enroll our daughter into the high school she would attend once we purchased the house. If you have moved frequently with children, you know that this is never an easy task. I went to the school, and the staff struggled to understand her International School records. It took patience and persistence, but eventually we gathered all the necessary paperwork, including proof of the purchase of our new home, and she was finally enrolled. After that, I became the daily chauffeur, driving her to school every morning and picking her up every afternoon for the next couple of months. It was exhausting but necessary, and I cherished the time spent with her during those drives.

We lived in the apartment for about two months while waiting for the previous occupants to move out. The complex was accommodating and allowed us to stay until the tenants were ready, although they held the upfront cash deposit.

Moving Day finally arrived, the day we had all been waiting for. The container with all of our belongings was delivered, and everything was carefully placed into our new home. To this day, of all the houses we have ever owned, this was my absolute favorite. We have a deep passion for U.S. history, particularly the colonial period, and this two-story colonial brick house fits perfectly with our colonial-style furniture and decorations. For our 25th wedding anniversary, we decided to have a re-creation of a typical colonial wedding. We conducted research and even contacted the Colonial Williamsburg Foundation, who graciously provided a full wedding ceremony and guidance on how the reception would have been celebrated in that period. Our youth pastor at church was more than willing to perform the ceremony in his black robe, guiding us through the "thee" and "thou" phrases throughout. We had costumes custom-made for this special occasion and even hired musicians to play harpsichord music on a keyboard and violin to complete the experience.

The reception included food and a cake that would have been typical of the colonial period. Our son and daughter were wonderfully supportive and played along with our enthusiasm, enjoying the day as much as we did. Everyone who attended appreciated the effort and enjoyed witnessing this unique celebration of our 25 years together.

Our son continued with his college life, returning to his campus and living in a "frat house," which we had never seen until the day of his graduation. I had always imagined it to be chaotic, picturing scenes like the movie "Animal House," but we were pleasantly surprised to find that it was a pretty clean and orderly house compared to our expectations. Within a few months, our daughter graduated from high school and began attending a college a few hours away, marking another milestone in our family's journey and the start of new chapters for both of our children.

My husband was now the focus of attention as the company began laying off employees who were 50 and older. Don't you just love it when companies decide you are too old to know anything anymore once you reach a certain age? Since he was already unhappy with the situation, he decided it was time to start looking for other opportunities. God always provides, and he was soon offered a great position with another company. Then 9-11 happened, and the world watched in horror as the events unfolded. Our world was forever changed that day, and it cast a shadow over everyone's lives in ways we couldn't have imagined.

We owned a place on the Florida coast, which we thought would be a perfect spot for our grandchildren to visit and spend time with us. However, when our son married his Prince from a Gulf Coast state, we learned that she was not enthusiastic about the beach or anything else about the property. Later, we decided to sell it, as it was too far away, expensive to maintain, and ultimately unnecessary since our son and his family were not interested in using it. Around that time, we were at the condo making some minor repairs when my husband received a call instructing him to return to work and lay off five of his employees. He asked why this was necessary, as he saw no reason, but companies were still reeling from the effects of 9-11 and were deeply concerned about their budgets.

He performed the sad duty, only to be called into the HR office a month later and told that the company could no longer afford his salary. He was given one month's pay and informed that it was his last day. Of course, this was not something anyone wants to experience, but at the time, God had blessed us with good savings, and he assumed he would have a new position quickly. In reality, it took two years before he found another job, which was eventually located in the Midwest.

Chapter 14
Trusting God in Hard Times

He went for the interview and was hired on the spot, which initially seemed a little strange to him. Later, he admitted he probably should have listened to his gut feelings and declined the position. But after being unemployed for two years, with savings running dangerously low, it is understandable that he accepted the first offer he could get. By this time, our savings had dwindled to nearly nothing, adding to the stress and uncertainty. He would call me with concerns about his new boss, but HR repeatedly assured him that everything would be okay. I decided to go and stay with him as we worked together with a local real estate agent to find a new home.

It was an emotionally difficult experience for me. I struggled with the thought of leaving my "favorite house" and now looking at homes that did not match anything I had envisioned or loved. The styles were different, and each part of the country seemed to have its own unique character that I had to adjust to. The process was both stressful and exhausting, but I tried to stay positive and focus on the new chapter we were entering, even though leaving the house I adored was heart-wrenching.

I loved the southern homes, especially the lovely two-story houses with classic colonial charm. I have to interject with a funny story here. I was in the agent's BMW as she drove me around to look at houses. You know how BMWs have a sensor that "dings" when the temperature drops below a certain level? Well, as she was talking, the sensor kept dinging. She turned to me and said, "Oh, don't worry about that, it's just telling me a certain time in Germany." She was completely serious! This was also the same agent who believed in placing "crystals" around a house to help sell it. What more can I say?

Just before I was to return home, we finally found a house we loved and put a contract on it. Then we had to put the "for sale" sign on our own house, hoping for a quick sale. My husband went ahead of me to start his new job in October, returning home for Christmas, but by that point, our house had still not sold.

Finally, it was another round of packing up and moving again. We arrived at our new home on February 1st, and the temperature was below zero with snow covering the ground. Being from the north, I knew how to drive in snow, but that does not mean I liked it. Snow is beautiful when it falls, but I want it gone by the next day. The moving truck arrived with our belongings, and the house was a chilly 32 degrees as the movers carried in everything. I immediately went to work unboxing box after box, organizing and putting everything in its proper place, while my husband started a job that was quickly dampening his spirits and enthusiasm.

We were in that house for approximately five months, and my husband became increasingly unhappy. He would come home at night, exhausted and frustrated, telling me stories about his boss, who was unpredictable, probably bipolar, and was cheating on company accounts. The stress was almost unbearable.

Finally, my husband decided he had had enough and reported the cheating to HR. Before you can say "shazam", my husband was told he was being let go. He was given two options: leave immediately or wait and be officially fired. Of course, he chose to pack his things up and leave right away. I went with him that evening as he gathered his belongings. We were escorted out of the office and to the door. Honestly, I was surprised they didn't just give him a literal kick in the pants on the way out. The whole experience was humiliating, exhausting, and yet, in some strange way, liberating.

So, there we were in the Midwest. We had just sold our house and had no clear idea what to do next. I remember sitting in the bedroom, overwhelmed with emotion, crying out to God, "Why does this keep happening? I don't understand. My husband is a good Christian man who is trying to make the right choices, and yet he keeps getting hurt in the end. My heart is heavy, and we have no place to go!" The weight of uncertainty pressed down on me. Since we had already sold our other house, we now faced the added burden of paying out-of-pocket moving expenses. Despite this, we were blessed to have found a wonderful church with an incredible men's group that encouraged and supported my husband. I am deeply grateful to those men who serve the Lord in such a selfless and meaningful way.

While we were still trying to figure out our next steps, we consulted a lawyer to see if my husband had any recourse. To our surprise, the attorney revealed that my husband was not the first, but one of many who had experienced similar issues with this particular boss at the company. The man had a reputation, and it appeared he had some kind of protection or connections. Unfortunately, there was nothing legally that my husband could do. Another heavy blow to our already distressed hearts.

Thankfully, we had maintained contact with some wonderful friends from our overseas days, loving Christians whom we deeply respected. I called one of them and explained what had happened. She immediately offered for my husband and me to stay with them while he looked for a new job. We ended up staying with them for two weeks, and the job market seemed a bit more promising than where we had lived previously. During that time, I went out with her real estate agent, searching for houses, and two days before we were set to leave, I found a spec house that was almost completed and available for purchase. You might wonder why we would take such a leap at that moment, but I can only say that the Holy Spirit was clearly guiding us. We knew we could manage the purchase, trusting that our house in the Midwest would sell quickly. With hope and determination, we drove home and began packing everything ourselves. Over the years, we had become excellent packers, having moved so many times during our marriage.

As we were in the midst of packing, our sales agent brought us wonderful news: the house had a buyer, and they were eager to move in as soon as we could get out. The family was from Chicago, had six children, and our large house was a perfect fit for them. Even more miraculous, they agreed to pay the asking price! Praise the Lord! I felt my heart lift with gratitude as I reflected on **Psalms 150:6**: *"Let everything that has breath praise the Lord."* We asked our son to come help us drive down to the new location, which would be a two-day drive. He was happy to help and flew out before the moving truck was scheduled to arrive, so he would be there when we left. Back in those days, he was such a kind and thoughtful young man, always willing to lend a hand to his parents and make the process easier for us. The day before we were to move out, my husband had a terrible accident while getting out of the shower. I heard him cry out in pain, and my daughter heard the fall from the next level of the house. It was a loud, heart-stopping thud, as my husband is a big man, and the impact reverberated through the house. I ran into the bathroom and found him bleeding heavily from the back of his head, with a pool of blood spreading across the floor. My daughter immediately called 911, and while we waited for the ambulance, I had to apply pressure to the wound to slow the bleeding. At the same time, I tried to put some pants on him, at least enough to be "decent" when the first responders arrived. I just couldn't imagine having paramedics enter with my husband completely naked.

Within a few minutes, five paramedics were in our bathroom, tending to him with professional care. My daughter and I followed the ambulance to the emergency room, where the doctors put seven staples in his head and instructed him to take it easy. Of course, this was particularly challenging because we were supposed to move the next day and begin our two-day drive to the new location. For the following year, my husband experienced memory issues; he could not remember his phone number, his address, and other important details, which caused us ongoing concern and anxiety. Eventually, a neurologist confirmed that he was okay, though we later learned that the ER should have performed additional tests to rule out a concussion. The incident left us shaken, but we were grateful that the injuries were not worse.

The very next day, the moving company arrived and efficiently packed all of our belongings. Despite the recent trauma, we headed out to our new location and new life with hope. God answers prayers in amazing ways, often in ways we cannot see while we are in the midst of a crisis. Only later, when we reflect on the events, do we recognize how He responded to the prayers lifted up to Him, guiding us safely through even the most difficult circumstances.

Chapter 15
The Wedding Woes

So, God has some interesting twists and turns for us. I sometimes think I know exactly what He wants, but other times I shake my head and try to figure out what just happened.

We were settled in our new home, we joined a wonderful church, and I got a job working part-time at the church, teaching preschoolers about Jesus for many years. It was wonderful to love these kids, to get to know so many parents, some of whom turned out to be lifelong friends. But mostly, it was such a wonderful opportunity to share the gospel with these children, some of them having no church background, and some with parents who didn't attend a church but liked the environment of a church preschool. After five long months, my husband finally got a consulting job with a consulting company. He traveled a lot, but at least he was working again. In fact, the first year he was with this firm, he traveled over 300 days out of that year! Wow!

It's at this time that our son is going to marry the Princess.

It's very difficult to know what is happening when only your son is trying to share the information the Princess wants to convey, but not directly to you. So, the wedding was being planned, and we were completely clueless.

So, the plans were being made for this wedding to occur in July, yes, the hottest month and also the time of hurricanes in the South. I believe the whole event was rather an omen when, on the day of the wedding, there was a major hurricane happening right over the event.

So, here we were, hundreds of miles away, and our son was telling us that they wanted the rehearsal dinner to be, well, we asked about a country club, a venue, a restaurant, where? Our son came back and said that they wanted it at a friend's subdivision clubhouse. There was no charge, and they wanted to have it casual and catered with barbecue, which was at our expense because this is the responsibility of the groom. Great! They would go ahead and get the catering service; however, since my husband had been laid off and we were trying to recover from our financial losses, our funds were limited. We asked that the number of attendees be kept to a certain limit. According to the rules, which we carefully referred to during this process, the rehearsal dinner is limited, but it was still enough for some out-of-town guests and local relatives and friends to attend. Everything I researched about the rehearsal dinner indicated that it is the groom's responsibility and intended for the wedding party only.

My good friend, who was gifted in planning such events, thought we were doing the right thing, which included the decorations, paying for the catering, and limiting the guests because it was a rehearsal dinner, not the reception where everyone could attend. OH NO! Years later, we were told that she and her family were still upset because some of her parents' friends from out of town were not invited due to the limitations we posed. Seriously! We did not have the funds to provide the event for everyone, but that wasn't the point. My friend had helped me, and we sought out Emily Post's guidelines for weddings, assuming we were doing the right things. However, we were later told that the decorations were totally wrong. The bride didn't like anything we did.

Also, my husband, who has a big heart, wanted to do something really special. I can't tell you how many hours he spent putting together an adorable video about the two of them, using pictures from the time they were babies up to their engagement (pictures we took, remember), and adding appropriate music to accompany the presentation.

Remember, he was working full-time and trying to put together something he had never done before, so it was not professional by any means, but he wanted to do it from his heart. Later, we were told that she disliked it and thought it was awful. Have you ever done something you thought would be so appreciated, something you put your heart into, only to be told it was terrible? The Princess is very good at hurting.

The next thing we did wrong was ask people to wear casual clothing, like jeans or even cowboy boots, as it was going to be a barbecue! However, when we arrived at the rehearsal at the church, all her friends in the wedding party were wearing strapless dresses, except for our daughter, who was wearing jeans. Oh yes, our daughter was in the wedding. From the time she first met the Princess, our daughter said there was just something about this girl's attitude that she really disliked. She did not want to even be in the wedding, but was doing it for her brother. I'm sure he doesn't even realize what a sacrifice it was on his sister's part to participate in this wedding that she clearly did not want to be part of.

The Princess and her entourage did not even include our daughter in conversation, not at the rehearsal, not before the wedding, not during the wedding, and not afterward. It was so bad that our daughter said even the bride's mother and sisters did not speak to her. We understood that their focus was totally on the bride and getting ready; however, rudeness is just plain wrong. There was no reason to ignore a person who was supposed to be part of the bridal party and who was about to become her sister-in-law. We are still amazed at how people can be so cruel. Yes, we understand it's "The Day of the Bride," but to not even speak a word to someone who was part of this event blows my mind. I know it hurt us all, but it was especially hurtful to our daughter.

The bridal luncheon was held at the house of the Princess's aunt, which was quite a long drive from our hotel. My good friend and her husband flew out and stayed at our hotel. She is one of the sweetest people I know. When we arrived at the house, the only person who came out to talk to us was the mother-in-law of the Princess's father. When it was time to go into the dining room to be seated, I found myself sitting across from one of the Princess's mother's friends from another state. Odd, I thought! My friend had been placed across from the bride's mother. Interesting!

I do believe that was all on purpose. What would you think? My poor daughter sat the whole time with the girls who had grown up with the bride, all best buddies, leaving my daughter completely excluded from the conversation. Even when she tried to join in, she was mostly ignored, which broke my heart to witness.

Chapter 16
The Princess Bride

What would you do in this situation if your princess behaved in this manner on her wedding day toward her husband, family, and friends? I think there was a show called "Bridezilla" which might apply here.

The wedding day arrived with hurricane-force rain and wind. My husband and I were getting ready, and I had this feeling of foreboding inside me. I can understand now why, as I felt like maybe this was the last event where I'd be able to see my son much again, just because of the events that had led up to this moment. We were barely out of the shower when our son called and said we had to be at the church early for pictures, and we needed to hurry up. Oh, great! So here I was, trying to dry my hair in humidity that must have been 150 percent, frizzing no matter what I did. We had the AC cranked up as high as it would go, and my husband was hot and dripping like me as we struggled to get all our dress-up clothes on and make it to the church.

We drove in heavy downpours with the wind blowing as if we'd be rolled over any minute, but we arrived really early at the church and stood around in the foyer, waiting for someone to tell us what to do. It was strange that we were the only two people standing around at the front of the church until our friends arrived and asked what was going on. The photographer came in, asked who we were, and even commented on what a beautiful outfit I had on. Thank you so much, as I had picked out a lovely satin long skirt with a jacket that was very pretty in pink and an accepted color from the Princess. Let me interject here that the colors I was told her mother would be wearing were completely different from what I was told when I had to go shopping for myself. Interesting, isn't it?

We waited and waited, and no one was coming. Finally, someone arrived and said that now we were to be included in the photos in the worship center. Guess what? They had all been in the worship center having photos taken, and we came in and had one picture taken as part of the group. I'm not sure, but I think we had forced smiles. Why did we hurry and wait for several hours before the wedding?

Since I'm telling you about the photos, I will also share that The Princess had a professional person making a video of the entire event. Later, during the first year of their marriage, we were asked about photos. We received a small memory book of the wedding and noticed that our daughter was not included in any of the group pictures of the wedding party taken outside after the ceremony. (Honestly, it was a miracle that God provided a brief time of no rain and low wind from the start of the ceremony until they left for the honeymoon.) Oh yes, they didn't bother to find her when the ceremony was over, and she didn't know where to go, so she went to the reception room to wait. Nope! They didn't come to find her to be included in the wedding pictures outside. During the wedding, the videographer was moving around, and I remember that as we stood outside waiting to throw our bags of birdseed, the camera person asked me a question while recording. Guess what? When we received this special "gift" of the professionally made wedding video, which included interviews of our son by himself and her by herself, along with the entire wedding, our son's family was not present in any of it. It was as if we had never been there. Remember, I said that she was hurtful? I always have to come back and remind myself of what God says: *"Love your enemies and pray for those who persecute you."* **Matthew 5:44**. I almost feel like, in her mind, we were "the enemy," for reasons most people would shake their head and wonder, "why?" She has never made a point to really get to know us, and honestly, we are very likeable people. Obviously, she has never cared to really get to know us.

The reception was divided. All of the princess's family and friends were seated on one side of the room, while all of my son's family and friends were on the other side. Not one of her family members who belonged to the church, and who must have known we were probably feeling a bit out of place, even bothered to come over and speak to any of us.

Some of our friends made comments about that fact. It was the weirdest reception I have ever attended. Our friends and family members were a bit shocked. I think what hurt me the most was how this affected my unsaved friends who had come to the wedding. After the bride and groom had gotten into their limousine, we turned around to go back inside, and all of her family and friends had disappeared. We guessed they had returned to the reception area, but no one bothered to include us. No one stayed to welcome us, invite us to stay, or even chat. Then my unsaved friend, whom I really wanted to experience a lovely Christian wedding, commented to me, "Wow, they just left you, and from what I've observed through this whole event, they are hypocrites; they call themselves Christians, but what horrible behavior."

We are always being examined by those who know we profess to be saved, but who themselves are not believers. Are we showing Jesus in us, in our lives, everywhere, all the time? I'm always thinking that I need to avoid being a hypocrite. I fail, I know, but at least I try to show Jesus in everything I do because that's what He expects of His children. I am still so bothered by this that this friend could see such behavior and, of course, decide that she doesn't want to have anything to do with Jesus if that is what He is about. I still wonder if her family did all this deliberately, or if they were simply being themselves and really aren't friendly or caring people. God is very specific about who is a judge, and I certainly cannot judge them for their behavior, but I do wonder what they would think if they knew what my friend said, and how they would feel.

Colossians 3:13 says, *"Bear with each other and forgive one another if any of you has a grievance against someone. Forgive as the Lord forgave you."* I had to remind myself of this every time I have been around The Princess and her family.

So, we traveled in the horrible weather for the next two days to return to our home. You know, this is the time when you truly leave your child in God's hands. You believe that your son has chosen the right person to be with for the rest of his married life. We always hope for the future that everything will be as wonderful as the movies on Hallmark.

Hope was all we had, and unfortunately, the situation between in-laws, now "out-laws", had only begun between our son and his new wife. Sometimes, we admit we may have said or done something that they took the wrong way or disliked, but we have never, ever been interfering in their marriage. Nor have we ever intentionally said anything that would be hurtful, mean, or interpreted the wrong way. We have never been "those interfering in-laws," nor have we offered advice to them. We have simply stated facts that always seem to be taken the wrong way.

But when you are suddenly told by your son that you are not doing anything right and that everything you say is "judgmental," then you begin to wonder. Where did that come from? You were never like that before you married The Princess. My son was always agreeable, and we got along great. He had always been appreciative of how he was brought up and the wonderful experiences he had growing up. Wasn't he the one who specifically wanted his parents to even come to his engagement? It didn't take long for her to have our son think we were outlaws, not in-laws, and he was not allowed to call or talk to us without her listening. How would you feel if your daughter-in-law put rules on your son about you? I shake my head sometimes when I think of all that she has done to hurt the relationship between her husband and his parents.

We really tried to have a relationship with them, but when you know from the start that your gut says the situation is not good, you start questioning the reasons for the behavior. What did we do wrong to make her act in such a horrible way around us? We tried very hard to be nice, not interfering, and not judgmental. We asked if they could share holidays with us since they lived very close to her parents. So, for the first (and the last) Thanksgiving we ever spent with them as newlyweds, he said they would fly out to be with us for a couple of days, and that they had to leave Saturday, after Thanksgiving Day, to be back with her family. They came, and she had headaches the whole time, sitting curled up in a chair or upstairs in the bedroom. My son came to us and said that she wanted to go to Black Friday sales because that was a tradition with her family. Apparently, she and her mom and sisters always went out shopping on Black Friday. We thought maybe this would be a way to get closer to her, even though it was not something we were really looking forward to doing.

We have never gotten up at 4 AM on the Friday after Thanksgiving to shop, ever! However, to show our love and good intentions, we all got up and headed to the mall. She and my son went off shopping and left us behind. Here, I thought that maybe this would have been a good bonding experience. Oh, right, I was not her mom in any way, shape, or form. My husband said he would never do it again, but he was doing this for them. It was obvious that she really didn't want to be with us. We got home, and she must not have had a good time because she stayed upstairs in the bedroom with a headache for the rest of the day, and then we took them to the airport the next day. I got a little teary-eyed and hugged my son goodbye, and she later said I was "too clingy and emotional." That was the last holiday we have had with them since they've been married. We asked ourselves, what did we do wrong? Why does she always behave this way with us? We have tried to go out of our way to be nice, friendly, and make her feel welcome, but she always makes us feel like we are horrible people. My son comes across as supportive of her but looks miserable, at least around us. He's always tired and worn out.

On another occasion, we asked them to meet us halfway at our condo to have a little bit of Christmas with them. Of course, this was not at Christmas because she always celebrates with her family. They drove to the condo, and she seemed to try to be friendly, but she always ends up being aloof. When it came time for them to open the presents, she opened a very nice gift (she liked Tiffany's, so it was special, I thought), but she looked at it and put it back in the box with no comment. I'm sure it was either not what she liked, or maybe it was just the fact it was from my husband and me. Oh yes, this is the bride who returned so many wedding gifts to a particular store that she was eventually banned from returning gifts there. Wow! It seems that it's hard to please this girl, and no matter what we do, she comes across as very ungrateful.

The Princess seems to know exactly how to push our buttons to make us look as bad as possible in front of our son. When there is so much tension in a room between her and us that you can literally "cut it with a knife," as they say, then you know it's bad. I remember several occasions when she just said or did something that made me want to lash out and ask her, "Why are you doing this?"

Instead, our way of dealing with her was to leave. We'd just make an excuse and go back to our hotel rather than stay around this person who clearly made it known to us that she did not like us.

Have you ever asked yourself if a person liked you because you just had a gut feeling they didn't? Let me share an experience from my friend, Susan. Her son was graduating with his second master's degree, and he wanted his parents to attend the graduation. He had to go to the university ahead of Susan and her husband to prepare, so he arranged for his new wife to drive them to the graduation ceremony. They had to arrive at their son's condo at a specific time in order to be there for the start. Susan and her husband showed up on time; however, The Princess was not ready and was hurrying around like a twister, ready to demolish anything in sight.

Finally, she was ready, and when they went to get into her vehicle, she told them both to sit in the back seat. Awkward? She acted like a chauffeur, driving herself and her husband for the distance of a couple-hour drive. The Princess drove like a crazy woman, going so fast that Susan was holding her husband's hand and praying God would get them there safely. She hardly spoke a single word to them, even though they tried to engage her in at least small talk. Apparently, she was so stressed about being late (which, unfortunately, is normal for her) that she had to concentrate on her speedy drive.

Upon arriving at the campus, she proceeded to call her son and tell him they were there, and then, instead of asking them to sit with her, The Princess went off on her own and left them standing there. At this point, her husband and Susan had reached their boiling points. How rude can a person be? Not to mention that this Princess had married their son and acted so horribly to his parents. It was not a good situation, and it was so bad that after his graduation, when they wanted pictures, she refused to be in any with his parents. Of course, Susan was not inclined to want her in any way, either at that point.

Needless to say, this is only one of the many ways she has been rude and downright nasty to my poor friend. Did they deserve this treatment? Honestly, they are a very nice couple, and they certainly did not deserve this hostility. Susan said she had to step back, look at what was going on, and just ask God for guidance at this point. They needed Jesus to help them be gracious and kind to a person who was definitely not kind.

Chapter 17
The Princess

I can honestly say that there are people in this world who, no matter what you do or say, will never accept you, and it can create more pain and anxiety than one person can handle. Does an incident or a person come to mind that helps you understand these feelings? It's just hard to explain, and some people won't understand the reason I'm writing this book or may even be judgmental about it, but there are many of you reading this who can relate.

I was having lunch recently with a sweet friend, and we were talking about our situation with my son. She said that she had been at a social gathering and overheard a husband and wife talking about their situation with their son and his wife, and she immediately thought of me. She said they were discussing how the daughter-in-law was a "princess" and how everything she was doing was so hurtful to them. Then she said something interesting that kind of clicked: "When a guy marries, his brain becomes her brain. He starts to think like her." I said she had something there.

I told her how my son was with us out in public shortly after they had married, and he wanted my attention. Instead of calling out "Mom," which he had always called me from the day he first spoke his first words, he instead yelled out my first name. I looked around and realized it was my son, who had always called me "Mom," not my first name. My first reaction was, "Was that my son?" Where did that come from, and when did he become disrespectful to me? To me, that was disrespect.

My husband and I had both noticed that The Princess was always calling her mom by her first name whenever we had been around her. So, I guess my son's now "connected brain" to hers thought it was perfectly fine to call me by my first name. Well, it might be okay with her mom, but it was not okay with me. I felt that this was the first time my son had been disrespectful to me. Since he married her, we have seen that change of disrespect extend to his parents. It's like an infectious disease that continues to grow inside him. The way he was brought up, taught to be respectful and tenderhearted, has now been influenced by The Princess. He has become unkind, cruel to his parents, and the most hurtful aspect of all is that he has become disrespectful.

My son and The Princess now have four children. I absolutely love children of all ages. They are so fascinating and often say the most honest and unfiltered things when they are little. So, it was with excitement and great anticipation that I looked forward to becoming a grandmother. I could hardly wait to hold that little one, and as they grew, I imagined all the imaginary games we would play and the countless books I would read to them, which has always been my favorite thing to do with children in the whole world. Having been a preschool teacher for many years, this was especially thrilling to me. The thought of holding my son's child and seeing that adorable face looking up at me was a dream come true. Grandparents live for the day they can be around their grandchildren, to play with them, read to them, and simply shower them with love. It's a special time in life, one we had long looked forward to. All of our friends who have daughters enjoy wonderful relationships with their grandchildren. We also know friends and family with sons who have great bonds with their grandchildren. However, there are those like us who live with hearts that are broken.

We wanted to see our first-born grandchild, fully aware that the visit would bring stress, but we were determined to manage it because we loved our son and wanted to love his child as well. How can a wife be so cruel as to prevent her husband's parents from adoring his child? How can someone take advantage of in-laws when they come simply to hurt them? We told our son that since we would be staying a few days, we would love to help out around the house, knowing how stressful it is with a first child. On the first day, my son handed us a piece of paper written in her handwriting, a list a mile long of things she expected us to do. I could immediately tell this was not my son's idea but hers.

As a Christian, I am willing to serve and do not complain when service is meant by both parties to be a good experience and a way to help each other. What bothered me about this list was that every single task was something she was fully capable of doing herself. I hope as I describe this incident, you will understand why it troubled me so deeply. One of the items was cleaning out her refrigerator. I was willing to do it, and I did, but I also knew this was the refrigerator that had never been cleaned in all the times we had visited; it was always in the same state. I don't know about you, but I cannot see how cleaning out a refrigerator constitutes reasonable help with the new grandbaby. I had hoped for time to hold the baby and let The Princess rest while our son was working a full day. Instead, my husband and I were basically relegated to the role of house cleaners, and our duty was to clean the entire house from top to bottom. We were also asked to paint certain things, tasks that I knew both of them were perfectly capable of doing themselves. I was brought up to handle things for myself whenever I was capable, so this expectation felt wrong from the start. I even remember her sitting at her computer while I was on my hands and knees scrubbing her kitchen floor. Yes, as a Christian, I knew I was to do this willingly and without complaint, but it felt more like a punishment. It seemed as though she took satisfaction in seeing me on the floor cleaning while she remained seated, unable or unwilling to lift a finger "in her condition." Would you do that to your mother-in-law?

My take on this whole situation was that I was being treated like Cinderella, forced onto the floor to do the dirty work for the evil stepmother. This trip turned out to be just as unpleasant as we expected, and perhaps even worse. Picture this: I was never allowed to hold the baby or change a diaper. When we asked if we could help with the baby in any way, she refused. She was heartless and cold toward us. Needless to say, this experience showed us what the future would likely hold and made it clear that our chances of having a normal, loving relationship with our grandchildren would probably be blocked by her. Our son is married to this person, and as much as we have tried to accept it, it is obvious that he feels either constrained or unwilling to push back against her. She could be a very controlling and cruel person, even to her husband, if he did not yield to every whim of hers. It is easier for her to refuse us than to confront the person she lives with twenty-four hours a day.

Our son asked us to come out for our granddaughter's first birthday. How can I even describe that day? When we arrived, The Princess, her mother, and her sisters were busy setting up an elaborate birthday party. I offered to help, thinking it might be a way to connect, but I was told I would only be in the way, so my husband and I went outside instead. When it came time for the birthday cupcake, all her family crowded around the highchair, completely blocking us out. I could not even take a single picture of my grandchild's first birthday with my camera. What was even worse was what happened after the cake. They all gathered in the living room and announced that our granddaughter would open the gifts from us first. Really? Why? Then, after opening our gifts, they said they would give her the rest of the gifts later in the evening, after we had left. I still cannot understand the logic of that decision, and honestly, it hurt deeply. It made me feel invisible on a day that should have been filled with joy, family, and love.

We were asked what we would like to be called as grandparents when The Princess was pregnant with their first child. My husband was giddy with excitement when they asked him because he said he had always wanted to be called "Pops." I said I would like to be "Grammie", a different spelling because I like things to be different. I'm quirky, I guess, about some things. They agreed to those names.

So, when she delivered at the hospital, we received pictures sent from our son that had been shared with everyone. The caption read, "The newest addition with mom, dad, 'GMa' and "Pops". Do you have any idea how my husband felt when he saw that her father had taken "Pops" as his grandparent name? I am sorry, but I can only describe that in one word: cruel. Why couldn't they have at least told us in advance about the names? We would have understood much better if they had communicated beforehand that her father wanted to use "Pops" as his grandparent name instead of letting us think that it would be my husband's name. It was so hurtful to my husband. He felt the sting of her nastiness. In my heart of hearts, I still wonder if events like this, such as the name, are deliberate, as they certainly seem to be to us. We have tried so hard to be understanding, but when things like this happen, your view of that person becomes very tainted.

Things began to get progressively worse. They never came to visit us, and we always got the excuse: "It's too far to travel with kids; it's too long a drive; it's too expensive." Oh yes, too expensive, but they could go on trips with her parents, go on cruises, and have fun as one big happy family. Yet when we suggested a vacation together, they refused. The hurtfulness behind their responses is that when we presented a suggestion, the reply was always "sure." But then, when it came time to actually make a reservation, the excuses started flowing like a fast-moving river after a torrential rain, and nothing ever came of it.

So, we have never spent a vacation with our son and his family. Maybe that was God's way of protecting me from a situation I could not handle. Contact became less and less frequent, and every time we asked anything, we were told it was "too demanding." Too demanding to want to see our grandchildren? Too demanding to watch our grandchildren grow? Too demanding to visit and spend time with them? Too demanding to just look our son in the face? We have friends who owned a timeshare in the area where their son and his family lived. They decided to visit, in part to see their son and his family. On a rare occasion, they were invited into the house to see and play with the grandchildren. They spent the day at the house; they were not allowed to take the children elsewhere, while the Princess stayed at her computer in another room or went upstairs to her bedroom.

Her son had worked a long day and was tired. The wife, on the other hand, had done nothing physically, merely sitting. When he pulled into the garage after a long workday, their daughter-in-law came into the family room, plopped down on the sofa, and put on a great show. Her son walked into the house, and nothing had been done; dinner had not been started. She placed her hand over her forehead in a dramatic fashion and announced that she was too tired and exhausted to possibly do dinner. This is just one of many performances they had observed from her.

On most occasions, this couple had watched their son come home from work, help make dinner, give the kids their baths, put them to bed, and then return to clean up the kitchen. Not only on rare visits did they observe this behavior, but their son had repeatedly mentioned how much he had to do when he got home or on the weekends and how exhausted he always felt. How does The Princess not feel any remorse about doing nothing to help? The house was always a mess. He had to cook most of the meals, empty or fill the dishwasher, and handle all the kids' needs as well.

I would love to help her understand, but I don't either. Adding to this, the counselor they sought for help remarked that one of the major stresses for their son with her was how untidy his wife was about the house. Interesting, isn't it? We had never said anything to our own son about his exhaustion from similar circumstances, but if we did mention how much he had to do, he would simply reply that there was not enough time. On another occasion, my friend and her husband went to their condo for a long weekend, and they asked their son if one or all of the grandchildren could stay with them for the night. The son and daughter-in-law even came to this lovely complex, which had a great playground, and inspected everything. Then they were told "no." They had no real explanation for why the answer was "no," but it was obvious they were not going to allow it to ever take place.

They were devastated that they could not spend some time alone with a grandchild, to have fun without her ever-spying eye on them. It's not like they would harm the child or let anything happen. My friend had been trusted by parents since she started babysitting at the age of twelve. All her life has been centered around children, and parents trust her, so why could this daughter-in-law not also trust her with the grandchildren?

They even asked if they could take the children out for a burger, and the answer was still "no." Could they take the grandchildren for ice cream? The answer was again "no." Finally, they realized the answer would never be yes. There were never any explanations for the refusals, just a flat no. When talking to other parents who experience these situations, they always ask themselves: Is it us? Their generation was raised to be thoughtful, kind, and respectful of parents.

I have read about why these parents are so different from my son's generation, but I wonder what God thinks about this. Can this generation be compared to the generation described in Hebrews: *"That is why I was angry with that generation; I said, 'Their hearts are always going astray, and they have not known my ways'"* **(Hebrews 3:10)**? Even though they profess to have a relationship with God, are their ways truly God's ways?

I know our son has been experiencing difficult times with health issues, the children's behavioral challenges at school, and job security concerns. I wonder if God is allowing these difficulties to get his attention. Maybe He is prompting him to ask whether his life reflects God's desires. I think it is pretty clear in the Bible what is expected in the relationship between a son and his parents, and it is heartbreaking to see these expectations so completely ignored.

Chapter 18
Broken—But There's HOPE

A few years ago, a couple took a cruise near their son's home, and they asked if they could visit. They also felt it was time to do something serious about the relationship with their son, so they requested to set up a counseling session with someone they knew and trusted. Everyone they knew had prayed so much and asked God to truly mend this relationship, as they missed their son deeply, but they also wanted to honestly be a part of their son's and their daughter-in-law's lives, as well as the children's lives. Have you ever prayed that God would just help you see The Princess in a different light, or soften your heart in a way that brings peace?

Son, daughter-in-law, and this couple were in full agreement, at least that is what he said, but they never heard it directly from her, that they should all sit down together. When they arrived at the office, she sat beside the son and did not say much. The wife can read faces pretty well, and she could clearly see on the daughter-in-law's face that she was not happy about this coming together. Finally, after several silent and uncomfortable minutes, they were asked to go into the counseling room for the session. They sat across from them in chairs, holding hands, while she and her husband sat on a very uncomfortable, very low sofa, which somehow made the situation feel even more unsettling and unbalanced.

For the next hour, they were told that they did not understand that their son had married her and that, according to the Bible, they were now "one," and anything and everything said or done was together. Actually, they did understand that right from the start and had never questioned that truth. Hadn't they all filled out forms from the daughter-in-law's church during the "before marriage" sessions in their pre-marital classes, carefully answering how they would like different situations to be handled by the newlyweds? They had even signed a contract with the church and before God that they would honor these commitments. These included things such as sharing birthdays, taking turns with each other's family holidays, visiting both sets of parents, sharing time with the children, and allowing grandparents to be part of their lives.

Then the son continued to go on and on about everything they had done wrong, repeating it in a way that felt overwhelming and relentless. The mother-in-law had always wanted to have a good and loving relationship with her daughter-in-law, so after the marriage, she wrote a heartfelt letter apologizing for anything she might have said or done that could have hurt or offended her. When she later asked her daughter-in-law about the letter, the response she received was, "Oh, I didn't even read it. I just threw it in the trash." What a painful moment. How unthinkable, dismissive, and deeply hurtful that was to hear.

However, the very worst moment came when the daughter-in-law said that she did not "trust them," and that was the reason they could not do anything with their grandchildren. She was completely crushed. My friend had worked with children all her life and had taught in public schools for many years. Those parents had trusted her to care for their children, yet her own son and daughter-in-law did not trust her? When she gently mentioned her lifelong experience with children, they responded that this situation was "different" and that they were not those parents.

Wow. This was coming from her own son, the one she had given birth to, raised, loved, and sacrificed for, and now his parents could not be trusted. They could not say one single kind or positive thing about them and instead kept repeating the word "demanding" over and over again, as if that alone defined everything. When the hour was up, she felt as though it had been one of the worst experiences of her life, leaving her emotionally drained and deeply wounded. It became painfully clear to her that nothing in that session had helped mend the relationship. In fact, it had made everything worse than ever before, leaving her with a sense that something precious and once whole was now truly broken.

The things that were said during the session were mostly bashing them, criticizing and attacking in ways that felt deeply hurtful. Finally, her temper got the best of her, and she looked the princess straight in the eyes and asked how she could call herself a Christian while behaving in such a hateful manner. Unfortunately, the session did not go as they had "hoped," and they left feeling now completely separated from them. Nothing felt right, and it seemed inevitable that the unresolved tension would only fester into further brokenness.

That night, when they went to their house to have dinner with the kids before leaving the next day, the princess had already left. She went to a friend's house until they were gone, waiting until the coast was clear. That counseling session ended up being the last time they saw her, their son, or their grandchildren. The daughter-in-law seems to believe that she was the injured party in that session, but honestly, both sides experienced equal harsh words and hurt feelings. Each side had said things in anger and frustration.

However, they did the right thing later by acknowledging that she and her husband had forgiven them and truly wanted to move forward, leaving the painful words of the past behind. Yet, like toothpaste once squeezed from the tube, words cannot be put back. The things that were spoken during that session could never be taken back or returned to their mouths, and the damage, the hurt, and the emotional scars left by those words remained, permanent and unerasable.

The couple even went back to the counselor two days later to discuss how badly the session had gone. She sat them down and explained that she had been counseling their son about his difficulty with an illness, something they believed was made worse by the stress when they were around each other. However, she emphasized that he is the one who lived with the princess, not them, and that she is very controlling and demanding of him. The counselor said their son was struggling with issues related to his wife, and that they all needed to come together to figure out how to help him cope with this disease.

Then, she shared the real reason she wanted to talk to them. In her words, she said, "You can't help a person who doesn't want or think they need help. Your daughter-in-law needs help but won't acknowledge it." She explained that, unfortunately, like many of the young women she had seen in family counseling sessions, their daughter-in-law had issues from her past, perhaps from her childhood, that she needed help with but refused to admit. She reassured the couple that they were not alone, as much of her counseling involved situations very similar to theirs with their son and daughter-in-law.

The counselor recognized that they were heartbroken, especially about the grandchildren, but she stated that she saw "no hope" for the situation ever getting better. Sadly, she was correct, because since that day, the princess has not spoken to them, and their son and grandchildren have remained distant since that session ended.

Time should heal all wounds, unless the hurt is so deep and there is no remorse for actions, or any consideration for others, especially from our own son and his wife. My husband has searched Scripture time and time again, seeking answers. One day, he said that we should follow what the Bible says about seeking out church elders to help resolve conflicts.

We sat down with a leader of our church and the now assistant pastor to the senior pastor, who happens to be our son's age. They told us that the situation would probably never be resolved. Instead, they advised us to pray for them and to continue telling our son that we love him unconditionally, no matter what is happening with his wife. They explained that there was no reason to involve their church elders because, given that her family had generations serving in that church, they would likely not take kindly to any negative words we might share. It probably would not lead to the resolution we hoped for.

They expressed sorrow for us and recognized how brokenhearted we were about the situation, but they honestly did not see any resolution until the hearts of our son and daughter-in-law changed. It was striking that their words echoed what the counselor had said, so we realized that we were hearing guidance from the Holy Spirit. The reality was hard to accept: there might be no resolution until their hearts changed. We just have to keep praying for them. The saddest part is the possibility that they may never change, and I may never see my son again on this earth while I am still living.

Forgiveness is sometimes hard, especially when it involves someone you love, and you cannot understand the reasons behind their actions. But Christ did something that changed the course of humanity when He died so that we could be forgiven. My husband and I have forgiven these acts of unkindness. As C.S. Lewis wrote: "To be a Christian means to forgive the inexcusable, because God has forgiven the inexcusable in you." These acts from The Princess are forgiven; however, she has not forgiven us, as evidenced by her actions toward us, especially her unwillingness to even speak to us.

Over the years, we have told our son that we have forgiven all the hurt and just want to move on. He has always said that they want the same, yet every time we have reached out to talk, he offers an excuse. She will not even give us a chance to speak with her by phone or in person. She has completely shut the door on us. I try to imagine what they are saying to their children about the absence of our presence and how that shapes their view of family. The silence is painful, and the longing to connect with our grandchildren grows heavier with each passing day.

As I write this, our son no longer reaches out to contact us. There was a time when he would occasionally set up FaceTime calls so we could see the grandkids, usually when his wife was away at her Bible studies. But even that small connection has stopped entirely. I read a saying recently that struck me deeply: "The things you hear as a child are written forever in your heart and in your soul." My mind often wanders to what they are telling their children about us, words that will likely be locked in their hearts forever. Are they telling the truth, that it is their parents who are unwilling to have a relationship, or are they presenting a distorted version, painting us as untrustworthy grandparents, incapable of love or care? The thought of those innocent grandchildren internalizing such ideas crushes my heart. How it aches when I think of those precious little ones who should be embraced by their grandparents' love.

The most painful incident, however, occurred within the past year. My husband's only aunt passed away suddenly, and we immediately flew out to attend her funeral. Coincidentally, she lived only a couple of hours from our son. When we arrived at the hotel, I sent my son a text, asking if we might at least see him and the children, knowing we were only in the area for the weekend. He replied that he and the kids could meet us at a restaurant the next day, but it would have to be at a specific time. I explained that with the funeral and all its obligations, I had no way of knowing exactly when we would be free, making it difficult to commit to a precise time. Ultimately, we were unable to meet, as the priority that day was my husband's aunt's family.

But it was clear to me that another factor was at play. When my son set a specific time, it seemed tied to his wife's schedule; he could only make arrangements when she was occupied and could not interfere with her plans. It became painfully evident that any contact with his parents had to fit entirely around her availability, as though we were secondary, if considered at all. That evening, I texted him again, hoping we could visit the next day since we were so close and would be flying home in just two days. I did not receive a reply until the next morning, which simply read: "Sorry, not a good day."

I was in tears, and my husband was both angry and deeply hurt. We sat together, asking ourselves why this had happened, and we knew the answer: The Princess. In my daughter's words, "she got to him." I believe that day stands as the most hurtful moment of my life at the hands of my own son. The fact that he could not take the initiative to make arrangements for us to visit at the hotel or find a way for us to see him and the children was unbearable. As a mother, the inability to see him, to hug him, to share even a brief moment together, tore at me. It had been years since we had seen him, and any chance of connection had been painfully denied, leaving a wound that continues to ache every single day.

My heart was broken into pieces by my only son. I think I finally understood a little of what Jesus was talking about when He said He was broken for us, that He was rejected by us. It is a horrible, indescribable feeling, and I know Jesus understood exactly how I felt because He became human and endured rejection Himself. Do you realize that my son has not looked me in the eye or really seen my face in years? Occasionally, he would text me on my birthday or Mother's Day, and once in a while might even call me from his car on his way home from work, the only place he apparently feels he can talk, but those conversations were always about how tired he was. They were superficial, distant, as if I were speaking to an acquaintance rather than my own child. In his text messages, he said he loved me, but I always wanted to ask him: How are you showing love, truly God's love, to your own mom and dad?

So, as you read my story and reflect on it, perhaps wondering if your son has married a "princess" as well, I want to ask you to consider what you would do in a similar situation. What do we do when our sons marry someone who is controlling, hurtful, and so demanding that even the husbands are prevented from having a meaningful relationship with their own family? How do we endure that kind of heartbreak while still trying to uphold love, grace, and understanding?

Just the other day, a friend and I were out shopping when she began telling me about her own "princess" daughter-in-law. She shared that no matter what she said, this woman always had a comeback, hurtful and demeaning, every single time they spoke. For instance, she mentioned her five-year-old grandson being "all boy," full of energy and curiosity. The daughter-in-law, who happens to be an early childhood teacher, looked at her and said something to the effect that "all boys and girls are the same, there is absolutely no difference between them." My friend and I exchanged a knowing glance, and both said, "Oh yes, there is!" Boys and girls are wired differently, perfectly and divinely designed by God for unique purposes.

It is incredibly difficult to remain kind and patient with women who believe they know everything, even though they have not lived our experiences or accumulated the wisdom that comes with decades of life. Yet, in today's society, it seems we are pushed aside, treated as though we are of no consequence, as if our knowledge and insight have no value. My friend confided that her daughter-in-law does not appreciate her at all, leaving her feeling dismissed, unseen, and disrespected in the very family she loves. This is the harsh reality many of us face when dealing with individuals who are controlling, dismissive, and lacking in empathy. The hurt is deep, the frustration constant, and the sorrow of watching our children's relationships change so dramatically is something that stays with us every day.

While reading a book recently by a lovely Christian author, I realized that much of what she described in her life resonated deeply with my own experiences. I cannot change the way The Princess feels, nor can I change the fact that my son married her. I know with certainty that nothing will change unless God intervenes and changes her heart. In the meantime, I pray every single day for my son, my daughter-in-law, and their children. I have come to accept that I may never be included in their children's lives, that I may never see them graduate, or be present for any special milestones or achievements they accomplish, unless she chooses to change her ways. My hope remains that someday the grandkids themselves will seek out my husband and me, longing for the love and relationship that has been withheld from them.

I recently celebrated a milestone birthday, and wow, it was a hard one to swallow. It is always difficult to face the reality of getting older, especially in a society that often disregards older people, showing little or no respect for the experiences and wisdom we have gained over the years. On that milestone day, my son did nothing more than text me to wish me a happy birthday. That was all. A simple, heartfelt conversation, a glance in the eye, or even a warm "Happy Birthday, Mom. I love you," was absent. The days ahead of me are inevitably shorter, and the past is in the past. I must focus on living each day as a precious gift from God, cherishing every moment I am given.

Just after Christmas last year, I finally asked my son to call me. He can only talk to me from his car while driving home from work. Isn't that sad? It is not a safe or ideal setting for a serious conversation; one is distracted by traffic, by the demands of driving, but if that is all that is offered, you do what you must. After discussing with my husband about the children's gifts, we decided we needed to know if the children had actually received them, since she apparently has a habit of throwing away gifts from us. Our son struggled to respond at first, but finally confirmed that they had indeed received our gifts. I remarked that I still wouldn't know for sure because we never receive an acknowledgment or a simple thank you. There was no comment, only silence.

Finally, I asked him point-blank if he could look me in the eye at that very moment and tell me that what he and his wife were doing to us was right. There was no response. Only dead silence. In that instant, I realized the painful truth: the reason he has not looked me in the face in years is because he knows, deep down, that they are not acting as Christians should, that they are not treating us according to God's direction for children toward their parents. He knows. Yet he is bound to The Princess, married to her, living under her influence 24/7. His commitment to her appears to outweigh any consideration for his own parents, and that reality is one of the most heart-wrenching truths I have had to face.

The hurt, the silence, and the absence of acknowledgment weigh heavily on my heart every day, yet I continue to pray, to hope, and to trust that God sees all and knows the desires of my heart for reconciliation and love.

How truly sad it is for all of us to endure being treated in this manner. Then he turned the conversation back to the past, bringing up the labeling of us as "demanding." What a painful curveball! As I have said before, they interpret our requests to see our grandchildren as demands, when in reality, all we want is to be a part of their lives, to do what grandparents naturally do. We want to spend time with our son, to witness the man he has become, and to nurture the bond we have shared throughout his life.

I asked him why he was bringing up the past when all we wanted was to move forward, to forget the old hurts, and to try to be kind to each other. Yet he simply cannot do it. My mind immediately went to the passage of scripture from Job 7:21, where Job says, "Why do you not pardon my offenses and forgive my sins? For I will soon lie down in the dust; you search for me, but I will be no more." As I grow older, I think about how my son would react if I were to pass away and he no longer had me praying for him and his family. Will he continue to harbor resentment for things we have tried to resolve? Will it even matter to him when one of his parents is gone from this world? Have you ever thought about this in relation to your own son? A friend of mine, who had lunch with me recently, shared that she lost her father suddenly. She said the most painful part would be the "regrets" that her children would have to carry for the rest of their lives. That thought struck me deeply as I reflected on my own situation.

In our conversations with our church leaders, they asked about The Princess's relationship with God, questioning whether she had truly been saved. There are people who claim to be believers, but in reality, their hearts have not been transformed. We want our lives to reflect Christ in everything we do. Even when our hearts are breaking, we strive to show true Christianity, trusting that God can give us peace in the midst of all the mess and confusion surrounding us.

Finally, I reached the end of my endurance. I was tired and worn out from trying for so many years. Do you understand now where I was coming from? You can strive to build a relationship, to repair what has been broken, but when it is clear that it is not going to work, and after years of trying, there comes a point when you must finally give up for your own well-being and sanity.

I absolutely love the writings of Lysa TerKeurst. I feel a deep connection with her when I read her books, as though we share a kind of bond through the experiences she has endured, experiences that echo my own over the years. God has gifted her with wisdom that I do not possess, yet recently, I received her book, *Good Boundaries and Goodbyes*.[1] This felt like a true "God moment" for me, a sign that everything I had said and done throughout these years was aligned with God's will. Holding that book in my hands gave me clarity and affirmation that I had acted under His guidance, and it finally allowed me to see that my boundaries, my efforts, and my love were all part of His plan.

He wanted me to understand the importance of placing a boundary between myself and my son, and why it had to be done for good reasons. Lysa Terkeurst addresses exactly what I had recognized between my son and daughter-in-law, yet I had been uncertain if the steps I was considering were correct. I would like to quote her here: "But if the issues are ongoing and continuously harmful, we must acknowledge that and act accordingly." She goes on to discuss how to put boundaries in place and emphasizes that good boundaries give us relief. She makes it clear that this is not only acceptable but also in line with God's guidance when done with the right heart.

My husband and I have certainly tried over the years, striving to maintain a relationship despite the repeated hurt. **Terkeurst** writes, *"And when you decide to establish boundaries and the other person (my son and his wife) labels you as controlling, difficult, or uncooperative, see it as a compliment. They are frustrated with you because you are no longer willing to participate in the unhealthy patterns of the past."* I had to read that passage several times to let it sink in, the idea that being called these hurtful names could be considered a compliment. Indeed, my husband and I have been labeled all of those words, and the resulting hurt and frustration have

---

[1] "Good Boundaries and Goodbyes" by Lysa TerKeurst.

eaten away at our very cores over the years. How can anyone, especially our own son, be so hurtful? I have cried my heart out, spent countless sleepless hours replaying the hurtful things they have done and said, and feeling the weight of their rejection.

Finally, after much prayer and reflection, and given the timely insight of this book, my husband and I realized that it was time to establish a boundary. We knew it was necessary for our emotional, spiritual, and relational well-being.

In my last conversation with my son, I simply said, "We've given you to God." At that point, we no longer expected anything from him and resolved that we would not reach out any longer. We were tired and worn out from trying to build a relationship that was continually met with resistance, and we were done. My husband and I continue to pray daily for him, his wife, and our beautiful grandchildren, whom we love dearly, even though we cannot see or talk with them. My son had nothing to say in response.

Then, almost immediately, he brought up again how "demanding" we supposedly were. Of course, there was a time he would never have said that to me, but clearly her attitude had rubbed off on him. It all comes down to perspective, doesn't it? What His Princess interprets as "demanding" is simply our desire to ask, not demand, for meaningful, quality time with our grandchildren and with our son.

Another painful example comes from my brother's family. His daughter-in-law has also been a true "royal princess," and as a result, they have had no contact with their son for twelve years and have never had a relationship with their granddaughter. They do know, through others, that her parents had moved closer to them. They had uprooted their home from birth to live near their daughter in another state. I have tried to understand why these women feel the need to have their parents so close by. As a daughter, I loved my parents deeply, but I was married to my husband and wanted to nurture that relationship while maintaining respect for my parents. We certainly did not feel it necessary to build our lives around being physically close to them. In today's world, with FaceTime and cellphones, it is possible to maintain strong family relationships without constant physical proximity. I don't understand the dependency that these princesses seem to have on their own parents.

My friend's son also married a Princess, and she has not spoken to her son in years. She has no contact with him, his family, or even the grandchildren, including a great-grandbaby. How terribly sad! Another friend has a son who has similarly cut off his relationship with her. I was at church recently and was asked what my book was about. When I explained that it's about our sons marrying princesses, she immediately shared that her son had married one as well. They had traveled many long hours by plane to visit him, but the daughter-in-law had packed up and left for the entire visit, never seeing them.

I speak with women who share similar stories, confirming the struggles I have experienced with my own son. My sister-in-law recently attended a gathering and overheard a couple discussing how strained their relationship had become since their son married. Another "princess," no doubt. What is common in all these situations? The sons have all married very controlling women who are selfish and indifferent toward their husbands' families. It is this selfish nature that causes such pain, and even those who profess to be Christians are failing to demonstrate Christlike love in their actions toward others.

So, What Do We Do????

To sum up all of this, here is what we can do: pray and read the Scriptures; trust God even in the middle of the mess; hope for a better future. Pray without ceasing. Do not allow the situation to control our minds and hearts. We must also choose to forgive. Forgiveness is essential, and we are called to forgive as Christ forgave us. All relationships require forgiveness to survive. If Christ can change lives, then I have to believe that one day, The Princess may learn to forgive as her Savior forgave her. We have asked for forgiveness from them, and we have made it clear that we have forgiven the hurt that was done to us. We continue to hold onto hope that one day hearts may change and healing may come.

We have had no response, no change in attitude, and not even a single word of "let's move forward." Nothing. Would that not hurt you? It hurts deeply. However, we have a God of love who cares for us. He holds my thoughts in check because they could easily spiral into bitterness, resentment, and dwelling endlessly on the different ways they have hurt us. Here is where my "hope" must be placed, in a future relationship with our son, daughter-in-law, and grandchildren.

Philippians 4:7 says, *"And the peace of God, which transcends all understanding, will guard your hearts and your minds in Christ Jesus."* I have to call upon His name countless times when my heart aches over my son, seeking that divine peace to guard me against despair and anger.

My husband and I miss our son deeply. I know my husband feels sorrow that his only son cannot even ask him for advice or simply talk father to son. Does The Princess even understand the hurtfulness of her actions and the influence her attitude has had on our son? We all try our best as parents. We fail; they fail. But ultimately, love is unconditional. I do not believe The Princess truly understands that kind of selfless, sacrificial love. I have no knowledge of whether her childhood was unhappy or if she experienced events that shaped her into someone untrusting of others. I do believe that childhood experiences profoundly influence how we treat people as adults. Therefore, I try to rationalize that she may not consciously realize the extent of her hurtful behavior, not only toward us, but also in dividing her husband from his family. His only sister has no relationship with her brother because of her influence. It is heartbreaking and undeserved, especially because she can be sweet and kind. However, our daughter, who is a keen judge of character, sensed this immediately. She did not like her from the moment they met, intuitively knowing she was a "Princess."

Why are these Princesses so controlling over their husbands? Why do they feel they can only nurture relationships with their own families and disregard the feelings of their husbands? Do they even care how brokenhearted the son's parents are because of their actions?

Have you experienced what I have, the soul-deep grief of being cut off from your own child and grandchildren? My heart aches. I pray to Jesus, and my spirit "groans" within me. Recently, I heard a sermon from Pastor and author Tony Evans about the Holy Spirit and how He intercedes for us when we pray. That teaching resonated deeply, reminding me that even in the silence and pain, our prayers are not wasted, and our hearts are known and understood by God.

I sometimes don't know if my words are correct when I am asking Jesus to help us with this situation.

Pastor Evans said that the Holy Spirit intercedes with the correct words from my soul, through the Holy Spirit, to Jesus. The Holy Spirit helps me communicate in a way I could not do on my own. My own words would probably be rather negative about my son and daughter-in-law, so I have to ask for a positive perspective, seeking how God can still work everything out for His good. I can pray with hope that someday they will desire the relationship we crave, and that we can experience the joy of being grandparents to our grandchildren.

I sometimes struggle with negative thoughts, and it upsets me that her parents are allowed to do all the things we wish we could do with the children. It seems even more painful knowing they spend Christmas, holidays, and birthdays with her parents and siblings, while we are denied the privilege, and I believe, the right, to have time with them. Our daughter-in-law once told us that it was a "privilege" and not a "right" to be grandparents. However, when our son married her and they had children together, I firmly believe that I do have that right. In these frustrating moments, I must turn to Scripture and listen to God's message for me.

I am often at a loss regarding how things are in these new kinds of marriages with these Princesses. I do not understand how someone can say one thing, then do the exact opposite, without remorse or guilt. I read in 2 Timothy 3:1, "But mark this, there will be terrible times in the last days." Is this part of what God was warning about, the separation of families, the hardships Christians may endure? I know this is something that happens not only to us but to many others as well. I have to keep looking to Scripture, asking God to heal me, and help me continue life knowing I may never see my son again. I pray that God will change the hearts of our sons and their Princesses before our time on earth ends or Christ returns.

I must remind myself to praise Him even in the midst of this situation. **Psalms 113:1** says, *"Praise the Lord. Praise the Lord, you his servants; praise the name of the Lord."* We have to put on the Armor of God to protect our hearts, so that we can still be a blessing to others by sharing our experiences. We serve a good God who only wants the best for us and desires to guide us through even the most painful circumstances.

Romans 15:13: *"May the God of hope fill you with all joy and peace as you trust in Him, so that you may overflow with hope by the power of the Holy Spirit."*

My hope in finishing this book is that you can find comfort in knowing you are not alone. May my life story serve as an inspiration, showing that God does care for you and me, and that He always brings us through the difficulties of life. I am amazed when I look back and realize how God knew everything before it even happened to my family and me. Even though going through those moments was incredibly difficult at the time, He has always been faithful.

I know there are so many others who can share similar stories, uplifting and encouraging each other along the way. My hope is that God will use me to be that blessing and encouragement for those of you who are seeking it, for those who feel alone, and for those who believe this is only happening to them; it is not. We are not alone.

We must keep the faith, looking upward and forward, not backward. May God be your constant source of comfort, hope, and peace. Blessings to you all!

Reflection and Discussion Questions

As you reflect on this journey, these questions are meant to help you process your own experiences, examine your heart, and seek God's guidance in difficult relationships. Whether you are reading this alone or with a group, take time to prayerfully consider each question.

1. **When have you experienced deep hurt in a relationship, and how did it shape your emotions and your faith?**
   Consider how that pain affected your view of others and your trust in God. Did it draw you closer to Him or create distance?

2. **What does forgiveness look like in your life when the other person has not asked for it or shown remorse?**
   Reflect on whether forgiveness is something you are holding back and what it would mean to truly release that hurt to God.

3. **Have you ever had to set a boundary with someone you love? What made it difficult, and how did you know it was necessary?**
   Think about the difference between protecting your heart in a healthy way and withdrawing out of pain.

4. **What does it mean to "give someone to God," and have you ever reached that point in your own life?**
   Consider the emotional and spiritual surrender involved in letting go of control and trusting God fully with someone you love.

5. **How do you handle negative or recurring thoughts about those who have hurt you?**
Reflect on what helps you redirect your mind toward peace, truth, and God's promises.

6. **In what ways can you continue to show Christlike love to someone who is distant, hurtful, or unwilling to reconcile?**
Think about what love looks like when it is not returned and how to maintain it without losing yourself.

7. **Do you struggle with unmet expectations in family relationships?**
Consider which expectations are realistic and which may be causing unnecessary pain or disappointment.

8. **How has prayer impacted your difficult relationships?**
Reflect on times when you felt the Holy Spirit guiding your prayers, especially when you didn't have the words.

9. **What does trusting God "in the middle of the mess" look like in your current situation?**
Think about where you need to release control and allow God to work, even when you cannot see the outcome.

10. **After reading this story, what is one step you feel led to take in your own life?**
Whether it is forgiving, setting a boundary, praying more intentionally, or letting go, consider how God is speaking to your heart right now.

About the Author

Natalie B. Sedgewick spent her career as an educator, and even in retirement, she still finds joy in tutoring children. Teaching has always been more than a job for her. It is something she truly loves.

Over the years, Natalie has lived in several states across the United States and even spent time living overseas as an expat. She has traveled to many parts of the world and explored countless ports on her cruises. Through all of her moves and adventures, she has built lasting friendships with women from all corners of the globe, the kind of friendships that stay with you for life.

When she is not tutoring or writing, Natalie keeps herself busy with crafting, painting, decorating, and reading. She has also been deeply involved in her church community, taking part in Bible studies, singing in choirs, and serving as a teacher and leader for youth groups.

Natalie lives with her husband, a proud Army veteran and a devoted husband and father. The two of them also share their home with their beloved rescued Schnoodle, who brings plenty of joy to their days.

Her children's books come straight from a heart that has always belonged to young readers.

Contact the Author: nataliebsedgewick@gmail.com